MYTHS OF THE TRIBE

WHEN RELIGION AND ETHICS DIVERGE

DAVID RICH

SECOND EDITION

ISBN 978-1-7322534-4-5

Cover illustration: Amy Hook-Therrien

Also by David Rich

Sail the World? – An Absurdly True Story, Prequel to RV the World

RV the World, 2nd Edition

Myths of the Tribe - When Religion and Ethics Diverge

Scribes of the Tribe - The Great Thinkers on Religion and Ethics

The ISIS Affair - Putting the Fun Back in Fundamentalism

Antelopes - A Modern Gulliver's Travels

Table of Contents

Preface

Religion is woven into the fabric of our daily lives and is integral to everything we do. Our belief in our religion determines whether we think we will survive this life. Yet there are approximately 4,300 organized religions, according to the statistical database adherents.com, which are further divided into more thousands of different denominations. The World Christian Encyclopedia, published by Oxford University Press, further separates Christianity into more than 33,000 denominations ranging from Baptists and Mormons to snake-handlers and holy-rollers. This book explores the historical foundations of religion and examines how it relates to ethics and morality.

Because of religion's highly personal nature, any discussion of religion is ripe with emotion. For many, religious faith answers the question of the meaning of life. Its close scrutiny tends to create anxiety, because such analysis is perceived as a challenge to basic beliefs. The obvious solution is to approach the subject with as little emotion as possible. Saying this, however, does not remove the difficulty, because when the stakes are this high it's difficult to excise emotion. Still, I will try to be objective by using, insofar as possible, universally accepted facts, assuming in 2019 that any facts are universally accepted.

One pitfall to this examination is language itself. The

meaning we individually ascribe to a set of words almost always differs. An illustration was provided by Bertrand Russell when he said, "I am firm. You are stubborn. He is a pig- headed fool." To avoid being characterized as a pig-headed fool when I only intend to be firm, I will use words carrying the least amount of emotional baggage. I will not, however, shy away from asking questions that require blunt phrasing. Before beginning the substance of this book, I invite you to consider an introduction by Robert Ingersoll to a speech he gave on May 8, 1888:

> "I am here tonight for the purpose of defending your right to differ with me. I want to convince you that you are under no compulsion to accept my creed; that you are, so far as I am concerned, absolutely free to follow the torch of your reason according to your conscience; and I believe that you are civilized to the degree that you will extend to me the right that you claim for yourselves."

We used to debate our important national issues, but now it seems we instead watch television and express unfiltered and undebated opinions on social media. The purpose of this book is to spur debate. We should read other viewpoints and debate fairly. If we disagree, we should respond carefully, rationally, and logically to those whose views differ from our own, so that we can begin a rational dialogue about institutions and ideas too long withdrawn from dialogue as sacrosanct.

Introduction

My kind have existed an instant in time, for a few thousand years, and are dwarfed in age by every other creature on the planet. The planet has been around ten thousand times longer than my kind. We're johnnies-come-lately.

The fish in the sea are my ancestors and have existed nine times longer than my kind. Our young still develop gills and a fishtail during the first quarter of their incubation. My fish ancestors enjoyed a lackadaisical existence, needing only to open their mouths for food and to swim moderately well. No other talents were necessary to life back then. When my ancestors were caught in twice daily tide pools and of necessity developed lungs, they were able to move onto solid ground and to encounter the traumas we've suffered ever since. It was no longer as simple as opening our mouths to obtain food. We had to hunt and scrounge for food and, on top of that, find shelter. Before our migration to land the surface of the ocean had protected us from all but the predators of the sea.

The dangers of the land consisted of far more than a hunt for food and shelter. Everywhere there were spirits to please, or the hunt would fail; predators, including others of our kind, would chase us from our shelter. To placate these spirits, we developed elaborate rituals that remain our

4

mainstay today. To control our fears, we sought control over the uncontrollable.

Early on we worshiped the cave bear, burying our dead with food, tools, and weapons for the next life. We watched out for spirits in trees, rocks, rivers, and animals and gradually began to worship mother goddesses and sun gods. These worshiping rituals would today be considered a combination of art, magic, and religion. Together they guaranteed eternal life so we would never die. This concept of eternal life made us superior to the other animals on the planet.

Every culture of my kind has thirteen ritualistic elements: song, exercise (standing, kneeling, bowing), exhortation, recitation of official texts, simulation (pretending), touching things, taboos, feasts, sacrifice, a congregation, inspiration, symbolism, and prayer. We call these rituals religion. Every group of my kind on the planet developed religions, all different but each deemed infallible. A particular religion may deny that its dogma is infallible, but none can identify which parts aren't.

Our earliest recorded history began in 1500 B.C.E. with the Golden Age of Amenhotep III in Egypt, though human writing extends back to 3000 B.C.E. Our history for the 45,000-plus years of our prewritten existence is based on archeology and myths. These myths are the basis for the world's religions, all founded after 1500 B.C.E. with the writing of the Hindu Vedas. Our recorded history is less than one-thirteenth of the time we have existed as a species.

During the first half of our 50,000 years of existence, three things occurred: (1) Cro-Magnon man moved west into the area of Europe, presaging Horace Greeley by 41,800 years. The Cro-Magnons founded the Cult of the Cave Bear, the world's oldest religion. (2) Neanderthal man succeeded Cro-Magnon man, and then died out 10,000 years later, to be replaced by true Homo sapiens: thinking man. The heroine of the book *Clan of the Cave Bear* was a Neanderthal who pioneered the replacement of the inferior Cro-Magnons. The Neanderthals died out 22,000 years ago. (3) Man crossed the land bridge from Asia to North America. These were the accomplishments of the entire first half of our existence—our first 25,000 years.

The second half of our existence was frittered away, with nothing improving the lot of the species until an additional 15,000 years had elapsed. Then a mere 10,000 years ago we racked up our next accomplishment and founded agriculture. Until we invented agriculture, thinking man had no time away from the daily hunt to think. Thus, after 80 percent of our existence had passed into history, agriculture began in the Middle East, in western Asia, or what is now Israel, Turkey, Jordan, Iraq, Iran, the Saudi Peninsula, and Egypt. Agriculture began soon thereafter in China and the Indus Valley of India, becoming our fourth major accomplishment. Jericho, one of our first cities, wasn't built until 7000 B.C.E., one thousand years after agriculture began. The first date in the Egyptian calendar is the equivalent of 4236 B.C.E. The traditional Christian date of creation is five hundred years later at 3760 B.C.E., or 4004 B.C.E., depending on whom you ask. This was when things started popping, 5,700 years ago, after 90 percent of our existence was behind us.

The Mayan calendar began in the equivalent of 3372 B.C.E. The First Dynasty of Egypt began in 3100 B.C.E. The Minoans founded Knossos on Crete in 2500 B.C.E. Stonehenge dates to 1860 B.C.E. Fire destroyed Knossos in 1400 B.C.E., making it the third longest surviving civilization in our history. The longest-lived civilization was founded in the Indus Valley, lasting from 3500 to 1500 B.C.E. The next longest civilization was the Egyptian, lasting from 2800 to 1085 B.C.E.

The Greeks destroyed Troy in 1193 B.C.E. In 994 B.C.E. David captured Jerusalem, the little town where we consolidated the myths of our species and founded three of the major religions of the world, hundreds of years apart. These three religions claim slightly over half of the world's religious people, all offering a personal god, which no other major religions do. The first to be founded was Judaism, in about 600 B.C.E., with 14 million adherents in 2019 and constituting a tiny fraction, less than a third of a percent, of the world's population. Six hundred years later came Christianity, which today claims 2.2 billion followers, 31 percent of the world population; and finally Islam, which can count 1.6 billion followers, or 24 percent of the population. Islam is projected to become the world's largest religion by 2060.

The oldest major religion still in existence is Hinduism, with a billion followers. Founded on writings accumulated from 4000 to 1000 B.C.E., Hinduism spawned Buddhism (now with 448 million followers) at about the time Judaism was founded. Christianity was a similar offshoot from Judaism. Rome was founded in 753 B.C.E. Buddha was born in 563 B.C.E. and Confucius in 551 B.C.E. Mohammed was not born until ten centuries later, in 570 C.E.

* * *

The belief in each religion's infallibility created major problems for the species. If a set of beliefs is considered infallible, then every other different set of beliefs must by definition be false and a blasphemy to the one true belief. A common solution is for the adherents of one set of beliefs to kill those who believe otherwise. From 1000 to 1808 C.E. up to 68 million people were murdered because of their religious beliefs; others assert that *only* a few million were murdered. No one knows the precise number, because the Christian churches destroyed records detailing the various

Inquisitions, which were far from confined to the Roman Catholic church. Sixty-eight million (or even half that) back then was a big chunk of the population. Throughout history, Christians have killed Muslims, and Muslims have killed Christians, and everyone has killed Jews. The killing was not of great concern to those who believed religious martyrs went directly to eternal life. Only eighty years ago another six million were killed in less than six years because of their religious beliefs.

We've become highly efficient at religiously justified killing, but the connection of these killings to religion has never become an integral part of the knowledge of the general population, because every country has a predominant religion which these facts would offend; accordingly, the facts are repressed from the history texts taught to our young. Religious killings continue unabated in many parts of the planet, including the Middle East, India, Africa, and other places where the religion of one country conflicts with the religion of a neighboring country or where there is religious conflict within the same country. Religious terrorism has become the name of the game.

In an educated society, value is determined by comparison shopping. Most people wouldn't shell out a hundred thousand dollars, pounds, marks, yen, or rubles for a house without looking at several and comparing their qualities. Most of us wouldn't spend a few thousand dollars for a car or a hundred dollars for anything without comparison shopping, but when it comes to religion and the theoretical preservation of our souls, few shop. Over 90 percent of us are converted to the religion of our immediate ancestors between the ages of twelve and fifteen, which is not an age known for wisdom and judgment. Our image of "God," according to an Emory University study, is formed as children and remains at that level of sophistication throughout our lives. Most never investigate the religion next door, much less any of our other thousands of religions. Perhaps to do so would be blasphemy to our immediate ancestors; yet, by the basic definition common to all religions, we commit without comparison shopping to a set of beliefs that determines whether we will rise from the grave, avoid reincarnation, attain enlightenment through basic truths, or pursue a hundred other paths.

Not only do few shop for a religion, few know enough to shop. In the United States we abhor the illiteracy of our children and associates in geography and history, but we know far less about religions or history than we do about popular TV shows, current movies, and our favorite sports teams. Jimmy Kimmel's 2018 interview of random folks on the street revealed that the vast majority are unable to name the title of a single book. Do even 10 percent of Americans know the difference between Judaism and Christianity, or Taoism and Buddhism? As a people, when it comes to both general knowledge and religion, perhaps the most powerful force in the world, we are collectively illiterate.

Some would argue that it is unrealistic to expect people to shop for values, that values are inherent in the culture and in our religions. But religion is not about values or ethics. It is about beliefs. If we are born in Iran our only god is Allah; if in India, our only god is Shiva and we long for nirvana; and, if in the West, our only god is the Christian god, with some obvious exceptions. As memorialized in a well-known hymn, "That old-time religion is good enough for me." George Santayana summed it up thus: "To me, it seems a dreadful indignity to have a soul controlled by geography."

The Facts of the Universe

What is humankind's future in the universe? How do organized religions relate to that future? Can we avoid self-annihilation arising from the antagonisms generated by our organized religions? To begin examining these questions requires that we be placed in our context in the universe.

The ability to judge anything accurately and intelligently depends entirely on putting that thing into context. We cannot, for example, accurately and intelligently administer justice without considering all facts surrounding a crime and putting those facts into context. Merely to know that the defendant shot the victim is to know little of ultimate importance. All facts must be explored so the jury can determine whether the defendant shot the victim accidentally, in self-defense, or with other justification. Without putting the accusations against the defendant into context, which requires knowledge of all knowable and material facts, we cannot determine whether a crime has been committed or its seriousness.

Similar considerations should be applied to organized religions. Religion in the abstract is incomprehensible; to understand religion, its historical role, and its relationship to ethics requires us to look at ourselves in context, which is to say, our place in the universe.

We know that our physical role in the universe is

relatively clear, based on elementary facts available in any grade-school science book. Specifically, the planet earth is so small and insignificant as to be meaningless. Write down the number of years you've been alive, and under that write the number of years you haven't been alive, which, beginning with the formation of earth, totals 4.6 billion years. Play with the two numbers. Add them or subtract them and see how much the larger number changes. As stated by the science-fiction writer Ray Faraday Nelson, "It gives you a measure of how much your individual life matters when we look at it in perspective, when we take, as it were, the Long View. It gives you a measure of how much my life matters, how much anyone's life matters." It could lead to the conclusion that the human lifespan is less than a flicker of light against the fabric of time. Yet the foundation of all Western religions places the earth at the center of the universe and humans as the ultimate achievement of "God." References to "God," "gods," or "god" are to concepts unrelated to the existence or nonexistence of a particular god, whether Christian, Muslim, Hindu, Greek, Roman, Egyptian, Sumerian, or any of innumerable others. Hindus alone have 330 million gods available to worship.

Our sun is one of an estimated 200 billion to 400 billion stars in our local galaxy, the Milky Way. Thirty galaxies make up the neighborhood of our galaxy and are so distant that most cannot be seen through our most efficient telescopes. Without a telescope, away from city lights and pollution, we can see only a fraction of our own galaxy and spots of light from three other galaxies, Andromeda and the two Clouds of Magellan galaxies. Thus, out of over two trillion galaxies in the universe, unaided by a telescope, we can see the lights of only four galaxies, including our own.

The primary difficulty in understanding the context of Homo sapiens in the universe is to understand a number as large as a billion or even a mere million. We can easily comprehend numbers we use on a regular basis, but these are small numbers. As children we needed no number over ten or twenty, and few adults, as a practical matter, use numbers over one million. The largest number in the Old Testament is ten thousand. The concept of one million was not even invented until the thirteenth century and is taken from the Italian term for "a large thousand." A billion was not invented until the seventeenth century, and even then, it was a curiosity without meaning. With the various national debts and inflation, a billion achieved practical meaning in this century but is not really comprehensible because no one can visualize a billion of anything.

Even if we could comprehend a billion, we still wouldn't have begun to comprehend the universe, because 200 billion (the lower estimate) is only the number of suns in our own galaxy, one galaxy out of two trillion galaxies in the known universe, and possibly ten times this many. To

14

arrive at the number of suns in the known universe requires multiplying the number of suns in our galaxy—assuming our galaxy is average—times the number of galaxies in the known universe, 200 billion times two trillion, which is 2,048,000,000,000,000,000,000,000, or 2,048 septillion, which is so far beyond our possible comprehension as to be ludicrous. In addition to the 2,048 septillion stars in the known universe, there are innumerable other celestial bodies, such as planets and moons and comets and asteroids. Yet, according to the ancient myths of our religions, the little proton of earth circling our remote sun is the center of "creation."

While exploring the sheer magnitude of many billions of anything, we should keep in mind that we haven't begun to define the extent of the universe, of which there may be an unseeable profusion. The meta-universe, or all there is, may be so much larger than the known universe as to be similarly incomprehensible; comparing the two may dwarf the size relationship between molecular and intergalactic structures. Our little earth and solar system may be a part of a side universe off a side universe that stretches its reflection through giga-universes in a billion mirrors through infinity. We may never know its limits until we can travel faster than the speed of light forever.

When one considers these facts in connection with Islam and Christianity, the two largest Western religions, it may be logically difficult to conclude that the creator of a universe with an immensity beyond our possible imagining sent his only son (do gods have sex or sons?) to die on earth, a tiny isolated orb, the third planet in a nine-planet solar system orbiting a star so minor that it is undetectable among the 100 billion suns of its own galaxy, a galaxy that is only one of hundreds of billions in the universe. The reason for sending the creator's son to earth was Eve's eating of an apple, which may be being eaten this very moment all over the universe. Does this mean that the Christian God's only son is traveling from insignificant planets in insignificant solar systems circling insignificant stars on the edge of billions of galaxies to die and hurry on to the next planet?

Our sun is thirty-three thousand light years from the center of the Milky Way galaxy. It takes the sun 225 million years (a cosmic year) to orbit the galaxy. The earth has made this orbit twenty-five times since it was formed 4.6 billion years ago, which was about 10 billion years after the universe began 15 billion years ago. To translate this into more understandable terms, if you were the first modern human (who appeared fifty thousand years ago) and were still alive today, you would have existed only two minutes out of a comparative year since the galaxy and universe were formed. Therefore, if God created the earth, he didn't rush into the creation of Homo sapiens. The Christian God, who created the heavens and the earth on the first day as described

16

in Genesis, used a day that was over 14 billion years in length.

Evolution takes time, and it never stops. Try to imagine what kind of animal Homo sapiens will be after another fifty thousand years. The probability is high that we will have evolved into a related but highly dissimilar (and hopefully improved) form. Kurt Vonnegut's *Galapagos* is a whimsical example of anticipating the immediate future of mankind. How different will we be after ten million years, ten times our current length of time on earth? Can we accurately speculate on the conditions of our existence and form after another 10 million years, which is only one thousandth of the time the universe has been in existence and three hundred times longer than mankind has yet existed? When God created humans in "his image," was that image reflected by Homo erectus, Neanderthals, twenty-first century humans, seventieth-century humans, or some evolution of humans yet to come? Or will we last long enough to find out?

If we are made in the image of a god, does that include Hitler, Stalin, and the other villains of history? Are there sadistic gods in whose image these men were cast? Which god is the image for racists, Ku Klux Klansmen, and terrorists? Is God's image that of composite man? These questions should be contrasted with the fact that we didn't practice agriculture until ten thousand years ago. How can we answer even hypothetically the question of human evolution and form a million years hence? Whose image will humans reflect then, or is God also evolving, and which god out of our thousands of religions is the true god? Does the image concept have any substance at all?

Should we expect God to be the epitome of logic and indeed perfect, eschewing political alignments? On the contrary, no god of any major (or minor) religion is either logical or morally superior to the highest form of human, such as Jesus Christ, Gandhi, Buddha, Mohammed, or Confucius, all of whom were nonviolent and nonjudgmental. None of the gods who head the religions inadvertently founded by these men (Gandhi founded no religion) are worthy of their ideals. These gods are routinely invoked by national leaders to justify mutual mass murder on both sides of any conflict.

* * *

Every species on earth is the result of evolution, and man as a species illustrates this fact as well as any other species. The fetal human heart begins with one chamber and then develops two like a fish, three like a frog, three and a half like a reptile, and finally four like other mammals. The same changes occur in our fetal blood, changing from fish blood to frog blood to reptile blood and finally to mammal blood. The salt in our blood and amniotic fluid is proportionate to the salt in the sea from whence we came.

We begin life as does all life, whether fish, frog, reptile, or dog. The facts of our embryology arguably illustrate our evolution and origins with more logic than a god theory derived from the notions of primitive humans.

Humans and apes represent a smooth, though not continuous, curve on the graph of evolution. Humans are not an out-of-character aberration but are similar to all animals.

Darwin described the relationship clearly:

> "All have the same senses, intuition and sensations—similar passions, affections and emotions, even the more complex ones, such as jealousy, suspicion, emulation, gratitude and magnanimity; they practice deceit and are revengeful; they are sometimes susceptible to ridicule and even have a sense of humor; they feel wonder and curiosity; they possess the same faculties of imitation, attention, deliberation, choice, memory, imagination,

the association of ideas, and
reason, though in very
different degrees."

Although fundamentalist Christian groups reject evolution, the Roman Catholic church accepts it. Because Catholicism represents the largest portion of the largest world religion, its definitions, as contained in *The Catholic Word Book* (reprinted from the *Catholic Almanac,* Huntington, Ind.: Our Sunday Visitor, Inc., 1973), will be used to *generally* illustrate Christian religious concepts.

For some time theologians have regarded the theory of evolution with hostility, considering it to be in opposition to the account of creation in the early chapters of Genesis and subversive of such doctrines as creation, the early state of man in grace, and the fall of man from grace. This state of affairs and the tension it generated led to considerable controversy regarding an alleged conflict between religion and science. Since the latter part of the nineteenth century, however, the tension has diminished, and today the Catholic view is that the author (or authors) of the Genesis account of creation wrote not as a scientist but as the communicator of religious truth in a manner adapted to the understanding of the people of the time. He used anthropomorphic language, the figure of days, and other literary devices to state the salvation truths of creation, the fall of man from grace, and the promise of redemption. It was beyond his competency and purpose to describe creation and related events in a scientific manner.

It appears that the development of humans, though linked cousin-like to the primates, is of a qualitatively different species, which should relieve people who don't wish to be identified as having evolved from monkeys. We didn't evolve from monkeys; we evolved separately and in parallel with monkeys. If humans become extinct there is little chance we would redevelop on earth, because our development was not directly related to the development of the one hundred other species of primates and appears to be a fluke of the first magnitude. Does this mean we were created by a god?

Evolution was taught by Aristotle and the ancient Greeks, such as Empedocles, in the fifth century B.C.E. Leonardo da Vinci wrote on evolution in code to avoid persecution by the church. The ancient Greeks and Romans deduced that the earth was round, not flat, and that it revolves, hundreds of years before Christ. This knowledge, however, was suppressed by the Christian church and survived only because the Muslim Arabs preserved it. The church persecuted the astronomers of the day because the Bible implied that the sun revolved around the earth, which was deemed the center of the universe because God stopped the sun and moon in Joshua 10:12–14 and backed the sun up in Isaiah 38:2–8. The works of Kepler, Copernicus, and Galileo were banned for 150 years because they were considered atheistic and heretical. However, in 2014 Pope Francis confirmed that the Catholic church believes in both evolution and the big bang theory.

Still, the banning of established science continues as an active and effective force in the United States. This force stems from fundamentalist religions and creationists who believe that God made all life on earth during one six-day week five thousand years ago, which tired God to the extent that he required a full day to rest. During the six days God worked he spent five days creating the earth and everything on it and less than one full day creating the other billions of planets around billions of stars in billions of galaxies and the balance of the universe. The creationists demand that this biblical "truth" be taught in our schools because they know that all science that disagrees with the five-thousand-years-ago date, when the earth, planets, stars, and galaxies were created, is malarkey, including geology, astronomy, biology, physics, and other basic sciences. In 2018 Arizona's top education official, the superintendent of public instruction, directed the science textbook committee to label evolution as a theory and teach creationism in Arizona classrooms while eliminating all references to the big bang and climate change.

The universal properties of the universe mean that life

is probable and widely scattered all over the universe. The level of its intelligence, however, is a separate question. Because humans observe the universe and are part of it, the universe, through man, is observing itself. Because dominant species inexorably grow in size, any civilization must expand and dominate (not necessarily destructively) its own solar system, then galaxy, and finally the universe, in order to survive. The reasons for this are relatively simple.

First, we have too few resources on earth to support our exploding population for more than a few hundred years because it doubles every thirty-five years. Our population is almost eight billion, expanding geometrically, primarily because of the general religious prohibition against birth control. In a hundred years our population will likely be 40 billion and in two hundred years 320 billion, which is sixty people for each one living now. We literally must have lebensraum, because by definition if we do not have room to live, we cannot live. Second, our atmosphere will eventually deteriorate so that carbon-based life cannot be supported. How soon this will occur depends on our efforts to control the loss of ozone and the buildup of carbon dioxide. At this moment these efforts look less than promising. Even if we are completely successful in ending all human-caused deterioration of our atmosphere, however, it will deteriorate by itself in a million years or so. With earth having been in existence 4.6 billion years, a million more years of life on earth is less than a hundredth of the time of our existence. Relatively, our species has little time left on earth.

Will we explore the galaxy and universe, or is this the stuff of science fiction? It's almost incomprehensible that intelligent beings will not eventually explore their environment and routinely travel over interstellar distances once the technology is available at a reasonable cost. If our survival eventually requires abandonment of this solar system, we have no choice. Thus, the eventual destruction of the earth's atmosphere may not be fatal to our kind. The foregoing is remote for one reason only: We may not survive our national feuds, religious wars, and apparently inherent greed.

A Brief History of Our Major Religions

"We are absolutely certain only about things we do not
understand."
—Eric Hoffer

A basic problem in examining religion is to make certain we similarly understand the terms used. Religious terms have no meaning outside their social context. The ideas of Buddhism have little meaning for a Western-civilization Christian, and Christianity is incomprehensible to an adherent of an Eastern religion. (Scientific principles, on the other hand, are as clear in Russia or Antarctica as they are in any other location.) Comprehension of religious concepts is impossible without knowledge of the particular religion, and extensive knowledge is usually required. In other words, there is nothing about any religion that is innate or logically necessary, though many religions have common threads.

Religion began in the caves of our ancestors. The first religion was naturalistic, worshiping the sun, the source of all life on earth. The sun oversaw all and brought warmth. The absence of sun was cold, darkness, and death.

The sun-god is a principal deity in many ancient

mythologies. In Greek mythology Apollo was a sun-god who fought to vanquish the serpent of night. In parallel Scandinavian mythology Balder was the sun who was in love with the maiden Dawn, yet he deserted her to travel through the heavens. They met at twilight and their tears of joy became morning dew. According to Hindu legend, Krishna was the sun, and at his birth the Ganges River erupted and life on earth began. Other sun-gods were the Persian Mithras, the Aztec Quetzalcoatl, and the Egyptian Horus. These gods were all born on the day when the sun triumphs over winter, on December 25.

Sun-gods often had divine fathers and human mothers who were virgins. The births of some were announced by the stars and attended by celestial music. Most were born in caves or other humble places, including Krishna, who was protected by shepherds. These common roots of religion were chronicled by a hero of the U.S. Civil War, Colonel Robert Ingersoll.

The tradition of tyrants stalking to kill divine figures is also common. All the babies in the neighborhood were killed when Krishna was born. The king sent his soldiers to kill Buddha, but a miracle intervened, making Buddha look twelve years old so the king's soldiers passed him by. King Typhon tried to kill baby Horus; the king pursued baby Zoroaster; King Cadmus went after baby Bacchus. Note the striking similarities between these ancient traditions and

Christianity:

- Sun-gods were born on December 25.
- Most were worshiped by wise men.
- Fasting for forty days is a common mythical motif.
- Many were violently killed.
- Sun-gods rise from the dead.

Jesus Christ is a sun-god. The Lord God of the Old Testament is the sun (Ps. 84:11). When Christians pray, they close their eyes, as do all sun worshipers. Even ancient man knew that looking directly at the sun would harm the eyes; hence the closing of eyes in prayer to any god of the sun. There is nothing original in Christianity. The Bible draws heavily upon religions and myths far older than Christianity or Judaism.

A pagan myth held Ceres as the goddess of the fields and Bacchus as the god of the vine. At the harvest the pagans made cakes of wheat, which they ate, saying, "This is the flesh of the goddess." They drank the wine and said, "This is the blood of our god." Similarly, baptism has not only been practiced by Christians but by Hindus, Egyptians, Greeks, and Romans.

The Brahman Adami and Heva were cast out of their Garden of Eden over four hundred years before the Christian Adam and Eve were thought of. The story of the great flood and resulting ark that saved a few Sumerians and two of each animal was written hundreds of years before Noah and his identical ark were penned for the Hebrew Bible.

The cross has been a central religious symbol since the ancient peoples of Italy, who buried their dead under its symbol before recorded time. The forests of Central America reveal ancient temples with carved crosses carrying bleeding figures. Babylonian carvings bear the symbol of the cross. The cross in ancient Egypt was a symbol of future life.

The Trinity originated in ancient Egypt, consisting of Osiris, Isis, and Horus, who were worshiped thousands of years before the Father, the Son, and the Holy Ghost.

The Tree of Life was found among the Aztecs and the ancients in India and China before the Garden of Eden was thought of. Other ancient concepts antedating the Bible include the Fall of Man, the Atonement, and the Scheme of Redemption.

* * *

The earliest religions, after our Clan Bear days, focused on the mother goddess, a fertility and nurturing symbol. The worship of these goddesses died out when we began agriculture about 8000 B.C.E. but reappeared all over Europe and Asia about 4000 B.C.E. The mother goddess is denounced repeatedly in the Old Testament as the sister of Baal, who in some early cultures was called Astarte or Ashtoreth and functioned as the center of legalized prostitution. Even though only Christians without sin are admonished to cast the first stone at a prostitute, prostitution has been prosecuted for the last one thousand years. Prostitution is considered a sin by organized religion because it is in direct competition with majority religious beliefs that prohibit birth control and sex outside of marriage.

A companion god to the mother goddess was the sun-god. An early sun-god was Mithra, whose cult was founded in Persia about 1350 B.C.E. Mithra became a primary god of Rome and was worshiped throughout the ancient world. The Catholic bishop's hat is called a miter, copied from Mithra's headdress. Japan, the land of the rising sun, is focused on a sun-god whose son was the emperor until deification was renounced by Hirohito after Japan's defeat in World War II. The prophesy in Malachi 4:2, promising a sun of righteousness, is interpreted as predicting the birth of Jesus, another sun-god. See also Revelation 21:23, which compares the light of the sun with God and his son. December 25 was the date of Mithra's birth; several Protestant hymns call Jesus the sun. Other sun-gods include Varuna, Krishna, and Vishnu. Christianity, therefore, fits into the mold of most older religions with a mother goddess and a sun-god begotten by a holy spirit. The story of the death of Jesus, his descent to hell (in the Apocrypha), resurrection, and ascent to heaven is identical to the story of Mithra. The common elements of Christianity and Mithraism include baptism, communion with consecrated wine, redemption, salvation, grace, rebirth, and eternal life. Other common elements are the wearing of fig leaves; the use of an ark to escape a world flood; a last supper by Mithra, which became a chief rite as the Eucharist; the presiding over a last judgment; and rebirth at the vernal equinox, otherwise known as Easter. Mithraism existed as a primary religion from 500 B.C.E. to 400 C.E. It continues today as part of most Western religions.

All human cultures contain parallels to the primary ancient gods. In the Bible Jehovah says, "Thou shalt not revile the gods"(Exodus 22:28, King James Version). Later versions of this verse were altered to reflect Christian monotheism: "You shall not revile God." Gods other than Yahweh (Jehovah) were spoken of positively in the Old Testament. By 100 B.C.E. these gods punished the wicked and rewarded the righteous with eternal life.

Except for the mention of "That One Thing" in Rigveda (the basis for Hinduism, compiled from 3000 to 1000 B.C.E.), the first monotheistic religion was Egyptian, established in the 1370s B.C.E. with Aten, a sun-god. Egyptian religious literature is similar to Psalm 104, Job 38–41, and other Old Testament passages, all written well after this time period. There are similar parallels between Egyptian hymns and New Testament passages in Luke 17:21, Matthew 11:27, and other verses. The Christian concept of God in man is the same as the Brahman, the universal self through Atman, the Egyptian concept of Aten, and the Tao in Taoism.

Christianity arose from Judaism in the way that Buddhism evolved from Hinduism. By the time of Jesus most religions were monotheistic, though many retained remnants of animism. Islam was primarily monotheistic when founded by Mohammed but retains major animistic elements, such as worshiping spirits in rocks, trees, other relics or fetishes, and particularly the black stone (a meteor) at Mecca. Catholicism is a modified monotheistic system with its trinity and numerous saints to whom prayers are offered, plus the Virgin Mary; it, along with general Christianity, features numerous fetishes and other animistic items of worship, such as the bread and wine of communion.

* * *

The oldest existing religion is Hinduism, founded in India between 3000 and 2500 B.C.E., though not organized and compiled into texts until 1500 B.C.E. Like all religions, its principles are hopelessly contradictory. Human sacrifice is commanded, yet it is a sin to crush an ant or eat meat. There are more Hindu priests, rites, and images than in ancient Egypt or Rome, yet Hinduism outdoes the Quakers in rejecting external trappings of religion. Central to Hinduism is the infamous system of four castes, the highest being the priests or Brahmans; then the warriors; then merchants, peasants, and artisans; and lastly, everyone else as untouchable. Whether a Hindu is reborn after death depends on karma; poverty and wealth, health and disease depend on karma or how the person behaved in a previous life. Christianity has a related concept with sins of fathers visited on their children and their children's children. Because one receives his exact desserts as a Hindu, the poor must remain poor, a teaching embraced by Mother Theresa.

Hindus believe that life is evil and obscures one's unity with the infinite, which is neither God nor any sort of god. Thus, Hindus must reject worldly things until they can become one with the universal self and avoid a perpetual cycle of rebirths. Unlike Western religions, Hindus seek an ultimate nothingness instead of an eternal afterlife and do not believe in "God." However, like all religions, there are sects and denominations that believe various details differently. Instead of allowing these differences to become divisive, most sects tolerate each other on the premise that no one has all the truth and thus no one is wrong.

Perhaps this concept is the most unique of any religion. Hinduism teaches, "Bow down and worship where others kneel, for where so many have been paying the tribute of adoration the kind Lord must manifest himself, for he is all mercy." Accordingly, Sri Ramakrishna became a Mohammedan and a Christian and concluded that all religions are equally true. Contrary to Christianity, Hindu gods live in temples, which are not places of worship. While the purpose of most religions is to overcome death, Hinduism, the third largest religion in the world with over a billion followers, seeks to overcome life.

Modern Hindu doctrines have introduced discontinuous reincarnation so that upon acceptance of Krishna as Lord, rebirths end. There are three primary Hindu gods: Brahma the creator, Vishnu the preserver, and Shiva the destroyer—another trinity of sorts. All Hindus stress yoga to achieve unity with self and block out the material world. A state of trance means unity with the absolute, which requires a personal guru. Unity with Brahma may be obtained by earnestly seeking him for three consecutive days, or seventy-two hours. Probably anyone would see God after being in a trance for seventy-two hours. In psychology this is called a self-fulfilling prophesy.

Hindu parallels with Christianity include rituals, bathing or baptism, scripture reading, and recitation. The Hindu creation is described in a book written over four hundred years before Genesis. The Hindu Brahma decided to make a world with one man, Adami, and one woman, Heva, on the island of Ceylon (now Sri Lanka). Adami and Heva were told not to leave the island, but a mirage created by the devil made the mainland look more enticing than the island. Adami and Heva, contrary to the instructions of their god, walked across a neck of land to the mainland, whereupon the neck of land disappeared, leaving them on sand and rocks. The Brahma cursed them to the lowest hell, but Adami defended Heva, saying it wasn't her fault, and Heva defended Adami, saying it wasn't his fault. For their selflessness, they were saved from expulsion to hell, but, as taught to all Hindus, humans thus fell from grace.

Another Hindu legend features a holy man named Menu who dipped water from the Ganges River and caught a little fish. The fish begged Menu to let it go. When Menu did so the fish warned him of a great flood and told him to build a huge ark to save his family and two of each animal on earth. Menu built the ark, and the flood came, bringing Menu's old friend the fish, which had grown to the size of a whale and had a horn on its head. Menu tied the ark to the horn and the whale towed the ark through the raging waves of the flood to a mountaintop.

Through even a cursory study of other religions we find there is nothing unique in the Christian religion or in any other religion; all religions originated with the superstitions and ancestral memories of our primitive ancestors.

The great flood may have occurred twelve thousand years ago at the end of the last ice age. According to physical geographer John Shaw of Queen's University in Kingston, Ontario, the last glaciers may have acted as vast blankets, melting from underneath and within because of the earth's heat. When the glaciers began to recede, water trapped underneath may have been released, creating a "massive worldwide flood," similar to that predicted by global warming. The flood is a folk myth in many societies, from Hindus and Christians to the Maori of New Zealand and the Native Americans of the Missouri Valley.

* * *

Buddhism is a modification of Hinduism and is the fourth largest religion. It's the principal religion in Sri Lanka, Myanmar, Thailand, Tibet, half of Japan, and much of China. There are more Buddhists in the United States than in India, where Buddhism originated. As in Christianity and Hinduism, the central evil for Buddhists is the desire for material things—a concept now studiously ignored by Christianity. Unlike Hinduism, Buddhism has no priests, rites, or creeds. Each Buddhist walks alone and can salvage himself only through his own exertions. There are Buddhist monks, but they are not considered priests; their only possessions are a saffron robe, a razor, a begging bowl, a water strainer, and a needle. There is no Buddhist church and no leader. The basic teaching is to follow the middle way between the world and asceticism. Both pleasure and pain are to be avoided. "Those who say, do not know; while those who know, do not say."

There are no Buddhist deities. The sole goal of Buddhism is to abolish desire and thus to attain nirvana. The four noble truths are life is suffering; desire leads to rebirth;

desire should be renounced; and the path of morality is eightfold. This path of morality consists of the right view or knowledge, right thought, right speech, right conduct, right means of livelihood, right effort, right mind control, and right meditation. Of course, few agree on what is right in any context.

Buddhists were the first ecologists, preaching selfless love for all living things, similar to Native American religions. Previous lives determine the present life's role; the key to life is self-responsibility. The three cardinal sins are sensuality/greed, anger/ill-will, and illusion/stupidity. Nirvana is not extinction but oneness with perfection when the fires of passion die from want of fuel. The Buddhist "bible" consists of three books: *Jataka,* which chronicles Buddha's 550 previous lives, twice as long as the Christian Bible; *Sutra Pitaka,* the sermons of Buddha; and a description of how to escape from the wheel of life.

All religions change to survive, though the changes are usually so gradual as to be almost unnoticeable; Buddhism is no exception. Buddhism in China and Japan is called Shinto. This schism formed by the time of Christ and now has many versions with about 50 million followers. One major sect is rational and ascetic, denying the existence of the soul or of God, and avoids the corruption of ideas by neither describing nor talking about them. Another sect is mystic and holds that nirvana is achieved by becoming and not by disappearing, that God exists but is beyond all human reason, and that all is illusory. Accordingly, any general description of Buddhism is necessarily inaccurate because of its many varying sects. In   China, for example, there are Buddhist priests who seek salvation for their followers but not for themselves. There is a Buddhist heaven that is achieved by faith and not by works; heaven is a paradise and not nothingness or the "incomparable misery" described by Hinduism.

Tibetan Buddhism boasts many monks, spirits, and demons; colorful pageantry and ritual; and a large dose of traditional Tibetan superstition. The Japanese version is Zen Buddhism, which is closely related to Taoism (25 million members) and Confucianism (20 million members). Zen Buddhism believes in revelation by sudden jolt, similar to Christian conversion, renouncing ritual, scripture, and vows. Its code of chivalry is militaristic and the fountainhead of judo, jujitsu, and archery. The proper course is the middle way between extreme positions, though like Taoism, Zen Buddhism is anti-education, believing that study and reflection lead nowhere except to confusion, a reaction against Buddhism. Japan purged Buddhism in the eighteenth century, adopting State Shinto with the acknowledged authority of the emperor, or mikado. The fanatical loyalty of the Japanese in World War II came from the cult of the divine emperor. In November 1990 several thousand

Japanese protested the enthronement ceremonies for Emperor Akihito on the ground that the state-funded ceremonies violated the constitutional mandate requiring separation of church and state. The many Shinto sects regard Mount Fuji as sacred.

* * *

Confucius was born in 551 B.C.E., making him a contemporary of Buddha, Socrates, and Pythagoras. Neither Confucianism nor Taoism espouses a hereafter: "While you do not understand life, how can you understand death?" In the belief that "absorption in the study of the supernatural is harmful," adherents conform to a philosophy that is as pragmatic as American capitalism. Their goal is to enjoy the simple life, especially family and friends, as opposed to acquiring material wealth. Confucius collected and rewrote many Chinese classical writings. His advice, as even Westerners know, is highly practical. For example, he said, "Do not think of all your anxieties; you will only make yourself ill." Confucius defined knowledge as knowing and admitting what we don't know. The yin and yang represent changing balances and circumstances in life. Five hundred years before Christ, Confucius posited the golden rule thus: "What you do not want done to yourself, do not do to others." This earlier version of the golden rule is easier to follow and arguably superior to the Christian version.

Confucianism recognizes an extended family with up

to 250 living members, featuring tablets of ancestors. By remembering their ancestors Confuscianists believe they are remembering themselves. Their sole religious function is the worship or veneration of ancestors. Except for a hundred-year interruption, China was ruled by Confuscianists for two thousand years, through 1910. This interruption was imposed when the Taoists briefly came to power until 141 B.C.E. Founded by Lao-tse, who was born in 604 B.C.E., Taoism is a pacifist doctrine teaching submission and humility, inaction and quietude induced by yoga breathing exercises to make the mind a blank. Taoism adopted the Buddhist gods, and there now exists a fusion of Buddhism, Confucianism, and Taoism, though their original doctrines contained basic conflicts. For example, Taoists are anti-education, believing that you should "do away with learning and grief will not be known," while Confucianism reveres learning. The resulting amalgam into Zen Buddhism is illustrated by two short poems:

Sitting quietly, doing nothing.
Spring comes and the grass grows by itself.
—Zenrin Kushû

We eat, excrete, sleep and get up;
This is our world.

All we have to do after that—

Is to die.

—Ikkyu

Chronologically, the next great religions were those represented by the Greek and Roman gods. The Greek religion, like the Native American religions, was based on agricultural myths, such as that of Demeter and Persephone with the planting and growing of corn. The Greeks adopted animistic entities, such as Eros, Fate, and Pan. The central gods were the Bright Gods: Zeus, Apollo, and Athena. The gods were indifferent to human quarrels and represented a combination of many local gods, uniting diverse tribes into a single people. The existence of slaves required the solace of religion so that slaves could bear their tortured lives, similar to the solace of a future existence promised by the Roman Catholic church to its poor masses. Then as now, religion was associated with public functions, which opened with sacrifices or prayers. Now as then, there is peer pressure for all to participate in these public religious functions, though no conformity in belief is required. The use of gods in the Greek theater was not considered impious. The oracles of the gods were consulted before war was commenced or momentous decisions made, similar to today when national policy is formulated over prayer breakfasts and, in the Reagan administration, astrological forecasts.

Rome adopted a system parallel to the Greek gods, with minor exceptions involving later emphasis on animism along with minor deities and spirits. The Roman system, like the Greek, was rooted in the family, with absolute authority of the father. Each occupation and each household object had an associated spirit or god. Janus was god of the door; Vesta, goddess of the hearth; the Penates, gods of the cupboard. All major events, as now, were marked by religious celebration: birth, death, puberty, and marriage. The entire ancient world believed in spirits lurking everywhere. The future was foretold by the entrails of beasts; by rain, thunder, and lightning; by magic, astrology, witchcraft, and miracles.

The Roman emperor was considered a deity, and there were several other underground religions, including the immediate predecessor to the Christian religion, the cult of Mithras. This cult was based on the Persian god of light, a sun-god, and was converted from being antagonistic to Christianity to becoming a part of Christian ritual and belief. The Mithras cult worshiped in underground temples that could hold fifty to one hundred people, with a sacred communion of bread, water, wine, and ritual.

* * *

The five great religions founded between 600 B.C.E. and 600 C.E. and surviving today are, in chronological order, Buddhism, Confucianism, Judaism, Christianity, and Islam. All are based on sacred scriptures. Islam and Christianity

41

feature a personal god, based on their antecedents in Judaism. The Jewish view is that God actively controls the destiny of a small nation, causing it to spread throughout the earth. Chosen people often become targets.

Judaism is based not on a single founder but on a series of prophets: Abraham, Moses, Elijah, Amos, Hosea, Isaiah, and Jeremiah. Both Jews and Christians claim that all prophets are descended from Abraham's second-born son, Isaac, including Jacob, Joseph, Moses, David, Solomon, and, for Christians, Jesus. Muslims agree with this genealogy, adding that Islam and its prophet Mohammed come from Abraham's first son, Ishmael. Muslims don't accept the idea of Jesus' divinity, claiming Jesus was instead a prophet on the same level as the other prophets and Mohammed.

The Hebrews were nomadic shepherd tribes that conquered agricultural Canaan, as ordered by their god. Their first recorded appearance, before their religious ideas coalesced, was about 1400 B.C.E. In 1005 B.C.E. their power was consolidated under David. Jehovah was a war god who defended his people in battle and against the Arab world. Judaism first combined ethics with religion, to the lasting detriment of ethics. Still, Judaism was a major intellectual development for that time, though arguably more primitive than the Code of Hammurabi (1700 B.C.E.), which was a refinement of older codes.

The Hebrews were exiled from Jerusalem in 586 B.C.E. and changed their name to Jews. For the first time Judaism became a personal religion. When they returned from exile, however, they excluded all foreigners and strictly prohibited intermarriage so that the religion (it is a religion and not a race, according to rulings by the Israeli Supreme Court beginning in the 1960s) became exclusionary. As in all religions, there are major contending factions. In July 1989, after the Israeli Supreme Court ruled that people converted by conservative or reform rabbis must be accepted as Jews and admitted to Israel, the Interior Ministry, which is controlled by orthodox rabbis, ordered marriage bureaus and burial societies nationwide to obtain certificates of orthodox conversion before performing marriages or burials. Thus, reform or conservative converts are admitted to Israel but are considered second-class citizens. The dispute over who is a Jew has made Judaism an increasingly closed society. Of course, many groups constitute closed societies but probably none to the extent of the Jews, who have been forever persecuted as a result.

Rome's dispersal of the Jews helped spread monotheism throughout the world, also facilitating the spread of Christianity. Orthodox Judaism today sees itself as a divinely appointed promoter of righteousness, designated to lead the world to enlightenment, though it has no missionaries. Like many religions, the central theme is the family. To the orthodox, the law is complete and infallible, which is a tenet of all Western religions. The more liberal reform Jews believe the religion is evolving and that Jesus is an ethical figure. The specific tenets of Christianity are rejected, but the spiritual and ethical ideals, and the monotheism, are the same.

* * *

Every aspect of European and American civilization has been shaped by Christianity, which began as a popular social movement by Roman slaves and the poor. The New Testament, however, admonished slaves to obey their masters, to repudiate violence, and to seek no earthly kingdom. Christianity is a combination of Judaism and Greco-Roman religions, which teach fidelity to the law. For example, the Book of Daniel is believed to be an allegory of Greek domination and the terror of Nebuchadnezzar four hundred years earlier. The idea of an afterlife was introduced in Daniel 12:2–3. John the Baptist was from the Qumran sect of Hebrews, which wrote the Dead Sea Scrolls; Jesus may have been, too. The Qumran, which stood for sons of light, lived an isolated communal existence, shutting out the world and its evil, the sons of darkness. Like all inadvertent founders of the world's major religions, Jesus never saw himself as the messiah. (See Albert Schweitzer, *The Quest of the Historical Jesus,* 1913.) Jesus severely criticized ritual religion and would have disapproved of today's Roman

44

Catholicism and all other Christian denominations, with the possible exception of the Quakers and similar groups. He rejected rank, pride, wealth, exclusiveness, and even formal prayer. The Coptic Gospel of Thomas, discovered in the 1940s, is a collection of the sayings of Jesus written between 40 and 100 C.E., closer to the time of his existence than the other four Gospels. According to the Gospel of Thomas, Jesus not only objected to formal prayer but said, "He who prays will be cursed." Jesus probably didn't author the Lord's Prayer.

Jesus' preferred form of economic system would have been communistic, communalistic, or pure socialism. Jesus had great contempt for political leaders who ignore the suffering of their people and announced his purpose to end conflict and establish a new kingdom of God, ending the quest for wealth and power. He said, "If thou wouldst be perfect, sell all that thou hast and give it to the poor and come follow me" (Acts 2:45). How many Christians have followed this central and explicit commandment? Jesus also said the rich, who in contrast to church members in developing countries constitute a majority in the United States, cannot enter his kingdom (Matt. 19:23 and Luke 6:24; see also, 1 Tim. 6:9 and Prov. 11:28). The religion closest to the teachings of Jesus is Buddhism.

Jesus would have disapproved of the current governments in the United States, Europe, and all capitalist countries. He would have been equally thrilled with the few remaining "communist" dictatorships and the other petty dictatorships around the world. There is probably not a government in existence today that would meet with his approval. Inflexible Western religions would have been regarded by the historical Jesus as no better than totalitarianism. Saul of Tarsus lifted Christianity out of its position as a Jewish sect and created a religion for the Greco-Roman world. Christianity became Greek in language and thought. As with all ancient religions it was founded on the idea of the seasons and rebirth after winter's death. Dionysus rose from the dead after three days, as did Attis, and became immortal. Christianity features a god who dies and rises again; its followers obtain immortality by oneness with and obedience to the god. All such gods are born of a virgin made fruitful by divine touch or breath.

The Christian creed was influenced by Pythagoras, who characterized man as a fallen god in need of purification, and by Plato, who emphasized a reality beyond the visible world. Knowledge of the supernatural was needed to explain the universe, the unknown, and evil events. The new Christian church culled out fringe rituals and fanatic ideas to form a simplified religion with orthodox ideas and order. Early Christians were fiercely intolerant of other beliefs, as their successors have been throughout history and as many remain today. Their persecution bred discipline and loyalty, and they gained widening power as the Roman Empire declined. In 313 C.E. the Christian religion was established as the official church and organized as a monarchy. As Hobbes observed in *The Leviathan,* "The Papacy is no other than the ghost of the deceased Roman Empire, sitting crowned on the grave thereof." The decline of the empire bred disorder, decay, and our thousands of "modern" religions.

The Roman Catholic church has 1.3 billion members, making up half of the Christian religion (Protestants number 950 million and Eastern Orthodox 270 million, all Christians totaling 2.5 billion). The next two largest religions are Islam with 1.8 billion and Hinduism with 1.2 billion.

The splintering of Protestantism from Catholicism was a gradual long-term revolt against the rigidity of Catholic theology, only to displace it with equally rigid Protestant theologies. The original impetus for Protestantism was the individual conscience, personal religious experience, and the right of private judgment with no priesthood through which the individual is filtered to reach God. The Catholic church exterminated those who wished to worship God directly.

A later chapter details the excesses of Catholics and Protestants against each other and among themselves during the Reformation and the various Inquisitions; here we touch only briefly on the skeletal outlines of the Inquisitions.

In 1176, Peter Waldo of Lyons founded the Poor Men

of Lyons, who were committed to giving their earthly goods to the poor, as expressly directed by Jesus. They were excommunicated in 1184 for arguing that all non-poor priests (a majority of priests), bishops, and the pope were corrupt. The pope ordered the burning of hundreds of these men, and many were smoked to death in caves where they hid. The Inquisition officially began in 1232 to stamp out the Poor Men of Lyons, the Albigenses, and similar movements. Entire cities were exterminated in Italy, Spain, and France, such as Beziers and Carcassonne. The Albigenses ("the Pure") rejected the sacraments and the pope, seeking salvation through repentance, self-denial, renunciation of marriage, and celibacy. These forerunners of Protestants, who were protesters in the truest sense, rejected the dual morality, wealth, and privilege accorded the priesthood, which was a corrupt lot. These reformers held that the Bible could be read by the laity and that war was immoral. This was considered blasphemy by Catholicism and treated accordingly. The idea of war as immoral is considered anathema by all religions in existence today, except the Quakers and a few other pacifists.

These early reformers included the Hus in Bohemia (Czechoslovakia), Wycliffe, and Martin Luther (1483–1546). The corruption of the Catholic priesthood was widespread. Many priests had concubines but absolved each other of that sin. They sold indulgences, forgiveness of sin,

48

to the highest bidder and conducted pagan rites. The early Reformation was an attempt to clean up the church and the priests' double standard, and to remove the church from political affairs. Luther and many others felt that religion without direct personal involvement was illusory. Luther formed an alliance with the ruling class against the peasant class, which he crushed, resulting in the slaughter of thousands.

The rigidity of the reformed Protestants was no better than the corruption of the Catholic church. For example, John Calvin (1509–1569) was unbending in all his beliefs, including those mandating church attendance and forbidding adultery or blasphemy. Violators were punished with death. According to Max Weber, however, the Protestant theology, with its work ethic, glorification of God, and frugality, became the linchpin for making capitalism work in the New World.

The Eastern Church split from Rome in the fifth century, but not until the watershed date of 1054 did the Eastern bishops refuse submission to Rome. The result was persecution of the Eastern Church by both Rome and the Muslims. The laity is far more significant in the Eastern Church than in the Catholic or the Protestant churches, with Eastern services conducted primarily by laity.

The Church of England and the Episcopal church are an amalgam of Protestants and Catholics, with issues separating the two main sects, such as whether bishops are the essence of the church (High Church) or just good management (Low Church). The Presbyterian church was established in Scotland with elected elders and was closely associated with the Congregationalists (now the United Church of Christ), who practiced pure democracy with no higher official than a local pastor. These separatists migrated from Holland to America, where they influenced the development of the U.S. government. Several state constitutions mirror the Congregationalist Constitution and the Mayflower Compact.

The Baptists took their name from the Anabaptists who, when founded in 1515, required adult baptism instead of infant baptism. In 1630, Baptist Roger Williams founded Rhode Island, which became the first state to grant complete tolerance in religious matters. The Baptists were divided by the Civil War, and to this day the Northern ("American") Baptists are separate from the Southern variety. The many other Protestant sects are based on their own view of the Bible and forms of practice, such as the Moravians, a missionary-oriented church. The Methodist church, with its circuit-riding preachers, is the second largest Protestant church in the world (after Baptists), with over 75 million members. Other unique sects include the Quakers, the Unitarians, and thousands of others. Much of Christianity is closer to the pragmatic teachings of Confucianism, except for the Confucian worship of ancestors, than to the teachings of Christ.

* * *

The last great religion was founded by Mohammed (570–632), who united the philosophies of Judaism, Christianity, and Zoroastrianism, amalgamating these with the desert religion of the Arabs, based on the Quran. The new religion served to consolidate the Arab nations into an aggressive military force that conquered Syria, Egypt, and Persia in the seventh century, then India, China, and Spain, and was finally stopped by Martel at the French border. Muslims occupied North Africa, then Sicily in 827, threatening Italy. Constantinople fell to the Muslims in 1453, which until then was a Christian stronghold, and it has remained predominately Muslim ever since. The Crusades sought to rescue Palestine from the Muslims, defend the Byzantine Empire against the Turks, and restore Christian unity. They failed miserably, due to disorganization, lack of planning, and factionalism.

Mohammed married the wealthy widow Khadija and sired Fatima, who in turn married Mohammed's cousin, Ali; their descendants are the Shia or Shiite sect. At age forty, Mohammed awakened to the God of the Christians and the Jews, attacking polytheism and animism, although to protect against evil, Muslims still worship spirits in trees, stones, and other relics or fetishes. Zoroastrian/Christian principles adopted by Islam include belief in the devil, angels, judgment day, hell, resurrection, the Old Testament (emphasizing Abraham and Moses), the New Testament, and the principles of early Christians. A principle charge of the Muslim religion is to expand by war and trickery based on its belief in "one prophet, one faith, for all the world." It is a Muslim holy war to kill unbelievers: ". . . kill them wherever ye shall find them." Christians, however, are not considered nonbelievers; the overwhelming majority of Muslims are not anti-Western. The Muslim concept of *jihad,* normally translated by Westerners to mean "holy war," actually means "struggle" in three separate contexts: ethics; justice and morality; and the fight against oppression of freedom and expression. However, like Christian countries, Islamic countries fall far short of their ideals.

Other principle Muslim beliefs include the duty of submission to one absolute god and an afterlife featuring seven compartments of hell for nonbelievers. Christians have their own compartment in hell, as do Muslim backsliders, Jews, Sabians, Magians, idolaters, and hypocrites, the last category creating a potential for overlap. The attributes of Islam heaven could tempt many to switch to Islam, with its promise of restored youth, joy, wine without harm, and an abundance of lovely women. It's unclear whether Muslim women will find fulfillment in such a heaven.

Islam permits no priests. Muslims regard the Christian Trinity as the worship of three gods, contrary to monotheistic principles. Islam means surrender to the will of God. The Muslim god hates oppression, injustice, usury, alcohol, and pork but is kind to orphans and the poor; the giving of alms is a central tenet. The religion is a simple one, intended for the common person, and does not seek, like Christianity, to elevate humans above their means or abilities. A common person can easily observe the requirements of Islam. The five tenets are recognizing the one god Allah and Mohammed as his prophet; prayer (unfortunately five times a day including before and at dawn, announced by one or more cacophonous loudspeakers); giving a 2.5 percent tithe as alms for the poor (primarily performed for Christians by their government); at least one pilgrimage to Mecca; and observation of the Fast of Ramadan. Things in doubt may be safely ignored. Be not envious. Expect sickness and death; don't expect sunrise or sunset. A simple, practical religion. Similar to Christianity, however, Islamic sects and countries stray far from the teachings of their founding leaders, lapsing into harsh and unforgiving fundamentalism such as that by ISIS in Asia and Africa, the Wahhabi in Saudi Arabia, and Shiite Iran.

All law comes from the Quran, including that governing the military, social life, and commercial dealings. The Quran, like the Bible, is a divinely inspired work. It was written by the angel Gabriel next to the throne of Allah on a tablet with rays of light. It's difficult to read or understand, however, consisting of a collection of disjointed sayings, the bulk of which are either dull or pointless, though there are a few gems of wisdom. The Quran is similar to the Bible, though not as bloodthirsty as the Old Testament. The Quran is zealously consulted and children are required to memorize large portions, which constitutes the bulk of their education. If there were no separation of church and state, Bible study would likely constitute education in the United States as it does in a few Catholic countries. The good advice in the Quran includes giving alms to others without public credit, loving your neighbor, honoring your mother by digging a well for the thirsty, and similar injunctions suitable for a desert people. Daily prayer is required, but the Muslim prayer is unlike Christian prayers, which primarily ask for assistance. The Muslim prayer is always the same: "God is great. I testify there is no God but Allah. I testify that Mohammed is the apostle of God." It's not a Christian prayer for help but praise to God with an unspoken request for guidance and forgiveness.

All Muslims are required at least once in their life to go to Mecca and kiss the black stone (animistic), a meteorite about seven inches in diameter, displayed on the outside of the Kaaba, a stone building twelve by ten by fifteen meters high. The Kaaba was erected by Abraham on the site where

God stayed Abraham's hand from sacrificing his son Ishmael (contended to be Isaac by Christians), signaling the birth of Islam. For more than thirteen centuries Muslims have been visiting Mecca at the rate of two million each year during a one-week period, creating crowds that would be unimaginable in the West. However, this overwhelming mass of people is unique, indicia of class being prohibited because the religion relegates all to equality before Allah (compare other religions). All wear the same attire, whether ruler or peon, rich or poor, black or brown, man or woman. Christians have no such once-in-a-lifetime obligation; the closest comparable obligations for Christians are wedding and funeral ceremonies.

Muslims are regulated in all things such as inheritance, dowry, divorce, and the treatment of orphans. Divorce is accomplished by the man's saying "I divorce you" three times (though a man in Malaysia was disciplined for divorcing his spouse by text). A man is allowed up to four wives if he can support them, plus slaves and concubines. Christians are allowed a wife whether support is available or not. Unless all Muslim wives are treated equally, only one wife is allowed. Mohammed's special revelations allowed him more than four wives by taking on the divorced wife of his son, in return for which he was required to avoid his concubine Mary.

The successors to Mohammed were the Caliphs, who

spread the word by the sword, similar to the Christians of the time. Mohammed's descendants live in Iraq (Mesopotamia), Iran (Persia), Saudi Arabia, and throughout the Middle East. Though Westerners may consider the Shiite fanatics in Iraq and Iran crazy, they're probably no more radical than members of other fundamentalist religions, Christian or Muslim. When right and wrong are black and white, arbitrary religious rules admit of no exception; our god is the only true god and all the gods worshipped by others are blasphemy to the one true god, no matter which of our thousands of religions.

The two main Muslim sects are the Shia or Shiite (Mohammed's descendants) and the far larger Sunni, which together constitute 80 percent of Islam, including ISIS and the Wahhabi in Saudi Arabia. The only Shiite countries are Iran, much of Iraq and Syria, and parts of Lebanon.

Westerners owe much to the Muslim religion. Without it we wouldn't have the writings of Plato and Aristotle, which were preserved by Arab philosophers when considered heretical by the Catholic church. From 600 C.E. to 1100, medieval Europe was backward while Muslims prospered, preserving scholarship and knowledge, flourishing in Cairo and Cordoba, teaching in the Greek tradition of logic and reason. Muslim scholars made all the advances in chemistry, physics, medicine, and algebra during this period.

Islam is making strides in Africa because of its comprehensible God, simple rules, and ease of obedience. Black Muslims are a lost tribe, representing the found nation of Islam, with notions of black superiority, similar to the idea of white superiority the West has held for centuries. Malcolm X's Black Muslims brought an international flavor to the civil rights movement in the United States. The twenty-first century, however, is a major challenge to Islam, because the religion's idea of civil society and the Quran are hopelessly out of date (witness its treatment of women). Muslims refuse to sign the United Nations declaration of civil rights because it guarantees the right to change religion. Conservative Islamic leaders, such as the late Ayatollah Khomeini, are paranoiac on this point and many others. The leader of the Iranian parliament publicly stated that the 1987 riots at Mecca, where over four hundred Muslims, mostly Iranians, were killed, was "a calculated plot designed by American and Israeli advisers to prevent the spread of the Islamic revolution to other parts of the world." More candidly, the Iranian leader should have said that Christians and Jews oppose the spread of Islam. Much of Islam is anti-Western but then much of Christianity is anti-Muslim. There are substantial Muslim blocs that are more tolerant of the West and are even allied with the West, such as Turkey, which until recently was becoming more secular with religion less important. Unfortunately, President Erdoğan

57

has become authoritarian and anti-secular.

* * *

Although Islam is a practical religion, it contains broad strains of mysticism drawn from Sufism. Christianity and all religions have this common core drawn of mysticism, requiring a genuine personal experience as the major turning point for the founder of the particular religion, whether Paul, Christ, Gautama Buddha, Mohammed, George Fox, or John Wesley. Each has exalted moments of intense emotional experience revealing that God exists and that God's existence need only be recognized to be felt. Devices ancillary to mysticism, depending on the tenets of the particular religion, include prayer, meditation, regulated and special forms of breathing, music, incense, dim or flickering lights, rituals, and prescribed posture. Some repeat sacred sentences or words and focus on sensuous imagery. Reasoning may cease and near catalepsy be reached, with or without visions, the hearing of voices, and the perception of light. Upon awakening there's a feeling of something special, though little or nothing of significance can be communicated. Sometimes the ritual creates erotic feelings, which may be one reason that adolescence is the usual age for religious conversion in the West. Trances revealing God are contained in various biblical passages (see Num. 24:4, 16; Acts 10:10, 11:5, 22:17).

Hindu mysticism emphasizes detachment from

58

worldly things. Yoga is the means to obtain detachment from all, to reach complete isolation, and achieve a soul devoid of desire. Sikhs also rely on yoga, chanting, stretching, and breathing deeply to reach the inner soul and "conscious rebirthing." Sikhs don't cut their hair, believing it releases positive electromagnetic energy. They instead cover their hair so the energy is harnessed and transmitted through the crown Chandra, or head, considered one of the body's seven major energy centers, to create a personal harmonic balance.

The state achieved by yoga is not dissimilar to the effects produced by the use of depressant drugs, such as alcohol or marijuana. An undeniable fact of all religions is their early and current reliance on hallucination-producing mechanisms, such as a severely restricted diet, breathing to the point of oxygen intoxication, dancing to exhaustion, flagellations, and the use of various drugs including alcohol (wine), peyote, cannabis, and mushrooms. Personal responsibility and judgment may cease. The result is an awareness of supreme enlightenment, which cannot be articulated, and which drug users experience similarly.

Many religious experiences (if not all) result from such mechanisms, including speaking in tongues and lengthy sensory deprivation in the form of meditation and prayer. For example, divine rapture originated from intoxication with drugs ranging from alcohol to marijuana, creating experiences indistinguishable from those labeled religious. Between a fourth and a third of people who take psilocybin (a hallucinogenic mushroom) have a religious experience. Does this experience prove the existence of a god or the "God" of any particular religion?

* * *

These descriptions of major religions and their key common elements apply similarly to the byways of religion, such as the Druze of Lebanon, the Assassins, the Fifth Monarchy Men, the Ghost Dance religion of poor Nevada Indians in the 1880s, or the cargo cults of Melanesia, where people built runways in the belief that a plane would come if they prayed diligently, bringing all their material wants, which is what got them started on the religion during World War II.

Gallup polls in the last decade have found that a third of Americans believe every word in the Bible is the word of God. A similar percentage believe in UFOs, while 44 percent of us believe in ghosts. A fourth (80 million) have received personal messages from God, and the same number believe in astrology. A fifth believe in witches, communication with the dead, and reincarnation, though Hindus in the U.S. are less than one percent of the population.

There are many other cults and sects that qualify as religions, such as Jim Jones's followers and the Moonies. Many attract older women with money who may find more camaraderie within these sects than with their children and grandchildren. In the northwestern United States three sects lured thousands of followers, such as in Yelm, Washington, where a 35,000-year-old guru Ramtha is channeled by a forty-three-year-old housewife. In Paradise Valley, Montana, a forty-nine-year-old mother of four claims to be the true vicar of Christ. In Medford, Oregon, a twenty-nine-year-old channels 2,000-year-old Mafu. Many elderly women have sold their property and given the proceeds to these cults. Exit counseling to wean their mothers from these cults has resulted in lawsuits by mothers against their children.

Other well-known sects include Jehovah's Witnesses, who believe in the immediate coming of Christ based on a vision in Daniel; scholars believe this passage actually is a disguised report by Daniel of current events in Rome and Israel. The Jehovah's Witnesses have eight million members worldwide.

A fundamentalist Protestant preacher, William Miller, gathered hundreds of his followers to await the end of the world in 1843; Miller relied on Daniel 8:13, which predicted the world would end 2,300 mornings and evenings after the fall of Jerusalem. "Twenty-three hundred mornings and evenings" was interpreted to mean 2,300 years after 457 B.C.E., the year 1843. When the world failed to end, Miller's followers gave him the consolation of becoming the Seventh-day Adventists.

The Hasidic Jews, a sect established in the eighteenth century, look for the Messiah and refuse to recognize the existence of Israel. The center for Hasidic Judaism is in Brooklyn, New York.

The Navajo religion is concerned with harmony in the community, the environment, and living one's life in contentment. Tony Hillerman described it as a concern with holistic health: "If you are not content then you are probably sick or you are going to be sick. Their notion is to restore the ailing person back to a state of harmony and beauty."

The Church of Jesus Christ of Latter-day Saints, founded in 1830 by Joseph Smith, is Christian but not Protestant, and observes many Christian tenets, such as the virgin birth, immortality, the Trinity as distinct "persons," communion, eternal marriage, and baptism. Other tenets are unlike mainstream Christianity, such as the baptism of ancestors and abstinence from tea, coffee, alcohol, and tobacco. Followers, known as Mormons, believe that God was a human who evolved into godhood and that those who obey the Bible and its equal counterpart, the Book of Mormon, will also become gods and goddesses, ruling their own world as God rules the earth. The second coming will occur in Jackson County, Missouri, where Christ will establish a New Jerusalem and rule for a thousand years. Polygamy was adopted by Mormon founder Joseph Smith but rescinded by God in 1890 so that Utah could become a state. It is Mormon tradition that their prophet Levi sailed from the Holy Land to the New World in 600 B.C.E. The Golden Plates of the Book of Mormon came from Moroni, whose father buried them in New York in 421 C.E. Joseph Smith was murdered by a mob in Carthage, Illinois, in 1844. Brigham Young moved the group to Utah, where they control state politics. They have seventy-five thousand full-time lay missionaries, eight times as many as twenty-five years ago, and sixteen million members, also eight times as many as twenty-five years ago. If you live in Utah (or Mesa, Arizona) and are not a Mormon, you have less possibility of political advancement and commercial success.

New Age religious groups include those who venerate crystals, believe in meditation with cats, or that they are aliens who've met Jesus, the Star of Bethlehem was a UFO, and Jesus was beamed up. Saul Bellow remarked, "A great deal of intelligence can be invested in ignorance when the need for illusion is deep."

The Origins of Religion

"One man's religion is another man's poison."

—Anonymous

The history of our religions is rooted in the fears and insecurities of primitive humans. The central appeal of all religion is the same: to fulfill the basic human yearning for security and personal control over our lives, which is obtained by ritual and other trappings of religion. Dr. Andrew Baum, a professor of medical psychology at the University of Maryland and an authority on survivors of disasters, states: "People have a need to explain misfortune. It seems too unacceptable to our species to believe that things happen randomly. . . . it's almost better for you to delude yourself," for without concepts such as fate and destiny to lean on, "we begin to lose our confidence in our ability to control the world."

Bertrand Russell in his book *Why I Am Not a Christian* argues that there are three reasons for organized religion: (1) the fear of death, (2) conceit that the members are a chosen people, and (3) hatred of those who fail to recognize the one true religion. Fear of death is a natural human condition; it would be unnatural not to prefer life. Conceit and competitiveness are also natural human characteristics as evidenced by our intense nationalism and religiosity, our capitalistic economic systems, and survival of the fittest resulting in evolution of the species. The resulting hatred of the "other" endangers the species by promoting unending conflict and wars among our many religions, which along with nationalism, racism, and greed cause much of the misery of the species.

The Concept of Eternal Life

Without the promise of immortality and heaven, which is offered in return for belief, religion would have little purpose, at least to the Western mind. The primary purpose of most Western religions is to escape death, the same hope that has driven man since ancient times, as evidenced by Neanderthal burials fifty thousand years ago with tools and food for the afterlife. At all times and in all places, humans have yearned for immortality, thus our early belief in animism and the powers of the dead, which has shifted to a belief in a power beyond death. This belief was central to the Egyptians. Their Book of the Dead promised that "thou shalt exist for millions of millions of years."

While Hindus believe they are reborn after death, for them rebirth is a punishment—which, in poverty-stricken India, has generally been the case since time immemorial. At the end of a good life the deceased moves up the food chain to a higher caste, eventually up to the level of Brahman. If the life was led badly the deceased must start at the bottom while awaiting rebirth on a nine-thousand-mile treadmill of burning coals in hell and successive hells. Nirvana is not the achievement of nothingness but of a true bliss, similar to the Christian heaven.

It's unclear whether there's an afterlife available in Confucianism or Taoism, except for the emperor and other nobles, though there does appear to be survival after death for some period of time as embodied in rituals of ancestor worship. On the other hand, neither has a conception of "God" but instead is oriented to almost pure pragmatism unrelated to an afterlife. The emperor was considered immortal until Hirohito renounced immortality. His successor, Emperor Akihito, was installed on the Chrysanthemum Throne in November 1990, after spending time cloistered with the spirit of the sun goddess Amaterasu, legendary founder of the Japanese nation. The government stated it was "not in a position to make any comment as to whether the emperor does or does not acquire such a divine nature."

Judaism could lay substantial claim to life after death. Witness Ezekiel 37, which is interpreted by Jewish scholars as portending the resurrection of Israel as a unified state, and the references in Isaiah 26:19, Daniel 12:2, and Ecclesiastes 12, the last mirroring the Egyptian concept of the soul's return to God. There is much in the Apocryphal Books on life after death; ancient Jews believed in immortality. The

Pharisees believed the body was resurrected, whereas the Sadducees believed that only the soul was resurrected. The Babylonian Talmud, circa 600 C.E., listed three hundred arguments for the resurrection of the dead. Orthodox and conservative Jews still believe in an afterlife, but without hell, for they also believe that death atones for earthly sins. Most Jews, however, believe this life is all there is.

The promise of immortality is central to the Christian religion, as illustrated by the most translated verse from the Bible: "For God so loved the world, that he gave his only begotten Son, that whosoever believeth in him should not perish, but have everlasting life" (John 3:16). Without this concept the Christian religion would likely not exist.

The mystery religions of Greece taught that the pure in heart would receive eternal life, a concept adopted by Christianity in Matthew 5:8. These religions used baptism to symbolically cleanse converts. Paul expounded Christian immortality in Acts 9:1 and 1 Corinthians 15:51–52. Mormons believe that most believers are destined for heaven, with the better Mormons becoming gods and goddesses who associate directly with God, lesser Mormons and regular Christians fraternizing with Jesus, and others mingling only with angels.

The ideas of Karl Rahner, a leading Catholic theologian, were summarized by Gerald McCool in two essays, titled "The Life of the Dead" and "The Resurrection of the Body," to describe the reasoning by which Christians believe humans possess a soul and are thus immortal:

> "Since man is an incarnate spirit, the human soul, even after death, retains its relation to the material world. Thus, the dead are still concerned with the evolution of the world's history. Man's ultimate future, his unity with the Trinity at the Parousia [the Second Coming], is a *human* future. Therefore, it requires the resurrection of the body and a glorified life in a new heaven and a new earth. So, Christ's Second Coming will be truly the glorification of his material creation.
>
> ". . . As we have seen, man is an incarnate historical spirit. Therefore, a purely spiritual union with God, a *Visio Beatica* in which man's glorified body would have no

part, cannot be the final perfection of man. Christ's victory, the triumphant result of his work in creation history, cannot have as its goal the disappearance of his material creation. Thus, those blessed men and women who share in Christ's triumph at the Second Coming will be fully human members of the perfect society which will live with the Incarnate Christ on His glorified earth."

Such reasoning requires many assumptions.

The idea of eternal life is inculcated into our minds as children, primarily to promote good behavior, much as children are admonished to be good if they want anything from Santa Claus, and it becomes an unshakable belief based on sheer hope.

Today's zoologists and biologists recognize that humans are in a real sense immortal. In discussing his influential book *The Selfish Gene* (1976), Oxford zoologist Richard Dawkins stated that "humans are nothing but temporary survival machines, robot vehicles blindly programmed for someone else's benefit." The reality of our immortality is manifested by the genes that replicate their exact copies through millions of years. We are here to replicate our genes; there is no other clear purpose in life, biological or otherwise.

Religion acts as a cultural unit of reproduction, which Dawkins calls a meme. Most religions are unconsciously controlled by the genes of their members, with the result that birth control is prohibited by most denominations within the world's four largest religions: Christians (overwhelmingly Catholic in numbers), Muslims, Hindus, and Buddhists. Similarly, there are no contraceptives in nature; the genes program the sexual urge, and we blindly follow, except insofar as we use effective birth control. Birth control is a primary individual means of control over personal destiny, which is one reason it is prohibited by our largest religions.

Basic human psychology tells us that we mentally experience whatever is necessary to cope with our fears and anxieties. When the stakes are as high as immortality and the opportunity to sit with the gods forever, extensive self-delusion and visionary experience is to be expected.

Superstition and Religion

Our first superstition originated with the Neanderthal belief in an after-life. We sensed spirits all around us, in rocks and rivers, in bears and beasts, in the wind and the sun.

70

We reasoned that if spirits inhabited inanimate objects, lower animals, and the forces of weather, we must individually have a spirit within us that lives on after our death. So, we buried cooking and hunting utensils with our Neanderthal dead, and our first superstition became the basis for Western religion.

Because there were spirits everywhere and life was unpredictable, we devised rituals to placate the unseen, to conjure favorable destinies and survival beyond the grave. These spirits explained lightning and thunder, eclipses and seasons, birth and death. Spirits gave warnings to animals, which eluded our hunt. It was otherworldly for a tree to grow from an acorn, so we explained the phenomenon by reference to spirits. Hardships and disease were caused by evil spirits that we learned to soothe through sacrifices and rituals. We elaborated our superstitions into sets of rules to reduce anxiety and make the universe seem predictable, establishing organized religion.

Astrology and voodoo, Catholicism and Judaism, lucky charms and rituals give us a sense of peace and control. Believers in religion profess to turn their lives over to God. Turning control over to another being, whether existent or not, relieves the individual of personal responsibility as long as the person follows the tenets of the particular religion, lucky charm, or ritual (such as in Alcoholics Anonymous). If these tenets are not followed then anxiety increases instead of being relieved. The religious solution is a rededication of our lives to whichever god is preferred by the particular religion out of the world's thousands of competing superstitions. If religious people were truly dedicated to God, the religious tenets would not have been violated and bad luck would not have befallen the faithful.

One primary difference between religion and superstition is that most of us are religious but most of us deny being superstitious. Instead, we "have beliefs" or "take precautions." The attitude of most is that "I have beliefs" and "you are superstitious." Both religion and superstition, however, are identical, belief in spite of contrary evidence and without any factual support whatsoever.

It is instructive to compare the practices of most, if not all, organized religions with the definition of *occultism* in *The Catholic Word Book:*

> "Practices involving ceremonies, rituals, chants, incantations, other cult-related activities intended to affect the course of nature, the lives of practitioners and others, through esoteric powers of magic, diabolical or other forces; one of many

forms of superstition."

Our superstitions and holidays are inextricably linked to our ancient religions. Horseshoes are considered lucky because the archbishop of Canterbury published a story in 959 about a blacksmith who shoed the devil with horseshoes, so a horseshoe above the door keeps the devil away. Horseshoes also deter witches, which is why witches ride broomsticks instead of horses.

Crossing our fingers mimics the ancient symbol of the cross; good luck supposedly follows. The pre-Christian version was a greeting by linking fingers, symbolizing intersecting spirits, a forerunner to the handshake. Crossing fingers into King's X was supposed to give immunity from a lie. Saying "God bless you" in response to a sneeze was originally ordered by Pope Gregory the Great in the sixth century when a sneeze during the plague foretold an early meeting with one's "maker." The number thirteen is considered unlucky because the Ides (usually the thirteenth day of the month) was viewed by the Romans as ominous.

The halo was originally a crown symbol. It was discouraged by early Christians as pagan but finally integrated into Christianity. The word *amen* originated in Egypt about 2500 B.C.E. as *amun*, meaning "hidden one," the name of the highest Egyptian deity. The Hebrews adopted it to mean "so it is," or "trustworthy." These concepts originated in our oldest religions and continue today as integral parts of society and our antiquated religions.

Many of the ancient rules of etiquette originated in *The Instructions of Ptahhotep,* the Miss Manners of Egypt circa 2500 B.C.E., and ended up as Proverbs and Ecclesiastes in the Bible. When the writing of the Old Testament began in about 700 B.C.E., these customs of etiquette had been around for eighteen hundred years.

Our spirits and gods are based on traditions and superstitions that date to an era before we measured time. These were natural mistakes and honest exaggerations made up by a species with a love for the marvelous.

The Roots of Religious Conflict

There are many good and practical reasons for religious affiliation. We conform to get ahead and make business contacts. Most of us fit on a continuum between church attendance to get ahead in business and true believers, with relatively few at either extreme; a graph of our religious sincerity would show a classically bell-shaped curve.

Catholicism explicitly recognizes the insincerity of some parishioners in the definition of contrition in *The Catholic Word Book*: "Sorrow for sin coupled with a purpose of amendment." Contrition for the purpose of hedging bets is called "imperfect contrition or attrition," which arises "from a quasi-selfish supernatural motive; e.g., the fear of losing heaven, [and] suffering the pangs of hell." Even bet-hedging contrition, however, is "sufficient for the forgiveness of serious sin when joined with absolution in confession." How many of us pay organized religion lip service because we might otherwise be shunned, fail in business, or fail politically?

The Positives of Religion

The average regular churchgoer is better off

psychologically than a non-attender, perhaps because the traumas of everyday life fall away when one is assured of a carefree afterlife. Similarly, strong commitment to a religious faith improves chances of good health. The religious generally suffer less heart disease and cancer. According to Dr. David Larson, research psychiatrist at the federal government's National Institute of Mental Health, "The more conservative they are, the higher the level of intensity of their religiosity, the more the health benefits." The primary benefit is reduced stress and depression. Seventy-five percent of widows are aided by their faith in religion and an afterlife. Religiously induced guilt (such as that experienced by the 17 percent of Americans who believe in a real possibility that they will go to hell) may outweigh for some the psychological and health benefits. However, for the terminally ill and disabled, religion is a great solace.

We know that hope, no matter its source, reduces stress and anxiety, lengthening life. A thirteen-year study by a Stanford University psychiatrist of the effects of psychotherapy on eighty-six women with advanced breast cancer concluded that talk therapy helped reduce their depression and anxiety, letting them come to terms with death. Women in psychotherapy lived an average of thirty-seven months, while those outside the group with similar diagnoses averaged nineteen months. Hope by itself is real; the source of the hope and its efficacy are unimportant.

Religious people who are unsure of their ultimate destination suffer increased stress and depression. Reality (particularly of certain death) for anyone, religious or not, can be depressing. As an antidote to general depression, religion ranks fifth and ninth out of the top thirteen choices, according to George Gallup's book *The People's Religion,* which catalogs years of Gallup polls. First in popularity for relieving depression is spending more time with television, reading, music, or a hobby; second is seeking out friends to talk to; third is talking to family members; fourth is eating more or eating less; and fifth is prayer, meditation, or reading the Bible. Ninth on the list is seeking out a pastor or religious leader, which ranks behind shopping or spending more, exercising more, and spending more time at work. It's the specter of death that attracts most of us to religion (including Hindus seeking to avoid rebirth); for the otherwise depressed, the remedies are more secular.

Another possible benefit of religion is its increasing involvement in social issues. For example, the National Association of Evangelicals states that the organization "represents evangelical concerns to the government and mobilizes evangelicals to engage in the public sphere. The NAE provides a forum where evangelicals can work together to preserve religious liberty, nurture families and children, protect the sanctity of human life, seek justice for the poor, promote human rights, work for peace, and care for God's creation." It also pursues a worldwide relief effort for "disaster response, child development, maternal and child health, HIV/AIDS, agricultural development, immigrant legal services, microfinance, anti-trafficking and refugee resettlement"—all wonderful programs, though of course many are available only to people who join the religious denomination that offers them. Other Christian sects are pursuing similar interests, including "Liberation Theology" in many third world countries, particularly in Central and South America. For almost the first time in our history religion is braving opposition to established government.

Some of this new social awareness arose from Vatican II, where the conferring bishops recognized that the church has historically been allied with the government in power, the middle classes, and the wealthy, though most of its members are poor. However, the primary social result of Vatican II was a declaration that priests and nuns should avoid the appearance of wealth and wear simple costumes.

A major benefit of religion is the sense of fellowship engendered by common beliefs, the formation of the "us." Pointing out that 80 percent of Catholics reject the church's stance against birth control, the outspoken priest and sociologist Andrew Greeley said that Catholics don't base their decisions about whether or not to remain Catholic on pronouncements by the Vatican concerning such matters as sexual morality. The deciding factor is whether or not they have become part of the Catholic community—whether it nurtures them and gives them a sense of belonging. These 80 percent naysayers receive Communion yet reject the teaching in a "sense that God understands the importance of sex in marriage, even if the pope doesn't." Greeley, who died in 2013, said he was "Catholic despite the Vatican and despite my cardinal." He believed that religion, like myth, symbolizes reality with poetry at its heart. This sense of community and oneness was illustrated by the reaction of thousands who were baptized simultaneously in Corona del Mar, California. A twenty-seven-year-old man said, "I feel loved. It's just a feeling in your heart. I can't explain it but you know it." A thirty-one-year-old woman said, "Now I won't feel empty anymore. Now I feel like I have a personal relationship with Jesus. It's wonderful." The sense of community was summed up by a thirty-two-year-old woman who said, "I can walk up to any one of these people and they are my brother and sister."

Some Americans are rediscovering religion. A wife raised Catholic and a husband raised Lutheran attended several churches after deciding "something was missing" in their lives. They gauged sermons, music, congregation size, and friendliness before choosing a Lutheran church that the wife described as nurturing "unbelievable friendships--spiritual friendships. We didn't really have any family in the area and I feel like these people are my surrogate family."

A Gallup poll found that half of all retirees expected "to spend more time seeking the basic meaning and value of life in the next five years." In response, many churches cater to a list of nontraditional needs, such as the $2 million gymnasium built by the First Assembly of God church in Phoenix, which features aerobics classes and a weight room, and the Community Church of Joy in Glendale, Arizona, which offers a counseling center with support groups for alcoholism, abuse, divorce, sexual addiction, and multiple personality disorders. A new member of the First United Methodist Church of Glendale said, "When I need it, it brings peace of mind more than anything, because I've always sort of had a fear of death. This gives me the feeling of something beyond death." The pastor of a Greek Orthodox Church with a 90 percent retiree membership said, "They seek honesty and integrity. It's a real community, not like a business or institution, which is something we're trying desperately to avoid."

The Downside: Us Versus Them

Religion for many is the primary positive connection with their fellow human beings in a stress-producing, highly competitive, and cold-appearing world. However, this sense of community has evolved worldwide into a syndrome of "us versus them"; those outside the particular religion are considered inferior, making it easier to engage in conflicts or war against inferior "others."

This downside in the formation of "us" is extremely serious, because it has splintered the world into thousands of factions battling for supremacy, converts, tithes, and influence, sometimes resulting in or exacerbating world conflicts. When George W. Bush said before the invasion of Iraq, "Behind all of life and all of history, there's a dedication and purpose, set by the hand of a just and faithful God," the same thing was going on in Baghdad as Saddam Hussein told Iraqi soldiers, "Fight as God ordered you to do." There have been few purely religious wars since the wars of Islamic expansion in the seventh century, the eleventh-century Crusades, and the sixteenth-century Reformation in Europe, but almost all wars have a significant connection to religious partisanship. For example:

- Christians versus Islamists in Afghanistan;
- Islamist Pakistan versus Hindu India;
- Islamist Eritrea versus principally Christian Ethiopia;
- Boko Haram in Nigeria and Cameroon;
- Al-Shabab in Somalia;
- The coastal Islamists in Africa versus the Christians in the interior;
- Shiites versus Sunnis in Syria;

- Palestinians versus Israelis;
- 9/11, and literally hundreds of others.

It's easy to understand why Muslims, Jews, and Christians have been at odds for hundreds of years, their conflict focused in the Middle East, where they began on the same small parcel of land. The Dome of the Rock in Jerusalem is a seventh-century mosque where Muslims believe Mohammed sprang to heaven on his horse. On the exact same spot, Jesus taught in the great temple originally built by Solomon, which was razed long before the Dome of the Rock Mosque was built. The Western Wall in Jerusalem is Judaism's holiest shrine. It's reasonable that any of these religions would wish to control their place of birth. Until organized religion disappears, peace in the Middle East is highly unlikely.

When Israeli soldiers killed Palestinian protesters in 1989, Iranian Parliament speaker Hashemi Rafsanjani suggested that "Palestinians retaliate [against] Zionist brutality with attacks against Americans and other Westerners and their interests around the world. If in retaliation for every Palestinian martyred in Palestine, they kill and execute—not inside Palestine—five Americans or Britons or Frenchmen, [the Israelis] would not continue these wrongs. [Palestinians should] hijack planes . . . blow up factories in Western countries. [Otherwise, Jerusalem] would not be liberated."

A month before this statement the Israeli army and police kept Arabs from attending Friday prayer services in Jerusalem, a day after Israel was condemned by the U.N. General Assembly for alleged human rights violations. The purpose for blocking Muslims from attending their services was to show Israel's control of its land. The killing of Palestinians and the blockade of the Gaza Strip has continued without interruption since long before 1989. Ninety-six Palestinians and seventeen Israelis were killed by each other in 2017.

Modern Christians also have difficulty living in peace in Northern Ireland, with its centuries of Catholics killing Protestants and Protestants killing Catholics. A visitor to Belfast or Derry could ask any two local residents how this began and receive diametrically opposed answers. The battle line pits Gaelic Catholic Ireland against Protestant England and loyalist Irish who are primarily Ulster Protestants. When the Republic of Ireland voted to join the European Economic Community in 1972, England suspended its government in Northern Ireland, recognizing that it existed only to serve Ulster Protestants.

Much of the enmity between the two religious factions derives from the Great Famine of 1845–49, when hundreds of thousands of poor Irish starved, and the Irish people blamed England for genocide. Sir Charles Edward

Trevelyan, who ran England's famine relief policy, felt Irish starvation was deserved as "the design of a benign Malthusian God who sought to relieve overpopulation by natural disaster." The Catholic survivors (whose population had been substantially augmented because of the prohibition against birth control) became dedicated enemies of their Protestant Anglo-Irish rulers, seeking to glorify their Gaelic Catholic culture. The tradition continues: Protestants are loyalists to England and Catholics are nationalists. When the 1937 Constitution of the Free Irish State was adopted, it provided the Catholic church "a special position . . . as the guardian of the faith professed by the great majority of the citizens." The clause was repealed by referendum in 1972, but no means were provided for taking Protestant Ulster into the Irish political mainstream. More than 3,500 were killed in Northern Ireland and tens of thousands injured, mostly civilians, before the Good Friday peace agreement in 1998. The casualties were, as in most wars, overwhelmingly civilian.

Brexit vastly complicated the status of Northern Ireland, because Theresa May's government was kept in power by a radical Northern Ireland party that may force a hard border between either the Republic and Northern Ireland or the entirety of the Irish island and the UK. The leaders of both sides in Northern Ireland want a referendum on unity with the Republic of Ireland. Brexit may have many unintended consequences and illustrates that when pure belief, the touchstone of organized religion, is the basis for any human action, our species suffers and society is diminished.

War has been waged in another part of the world for over thirty years, but few Westerners have heard of it. At stake is the possession of the Siachen, one thousand square miles of glaciated wasteland in the Himalayas between Pakistan-occupied Kashmir and Chinese territory. The combatants are Indian Hindus and Pakistani Muslims. Conditions are so harsh that only a third of the casualties are due to combat. The fighting occurs at altitudes above nineteen thousand feet in knee-deep snow, over two-hundred-foot crevasses, and on walls of ice where temperatures frequently drop below minus fifty degrees. Soldiers carry sixty-five-pound packs, ice picks, skis, shovels, and ropes, and before leaving for combat both sides visit their respective enclaves, where either images of the Hindu gods Rama, Shiva, and Ganesh have been hung by the Indian troops or the holy symbols of the Muslim god have been hung by the Pakistani troops.

The civil war in Syria began in 2011 with al-Assad's minority Alawites allied with Iran's Shi'a government against the country's Sunni majority (87–90 percent of Islam) and Turkey's Sunni government, complicated by Syria's many religious minorities including Kurds, Yazidi,

Christians, and of course, ISIS, fundamentalist Sunnis.

After writing the first edition of this book my wife and I traveled in 170 countries, witnessing the world's religious hatreds up close and intimately. (See my book *The ISIS Affair.*) The animosity between Sunnis and Shi'a parallels the Christian Inquisitions. Both sides despise the other; this observation is based on my experience living in Pakistan, Yemen, Indonesia, and the former Soviet republics of Uzbekistan, Kyrgyzstan, Tajikistan, Azerbaijan, and Turkmenistan. The animosity between Christians and Muslims in Africa is equally intense. Witness Boko Haram in Nigeria and Cameroon, and al-Shabaab in Somalia and Kenya.

East Timor, a former Portuguese colony on an island off the north coast of Australia, suffered a religious war when Indonesian Muslims invaded in 1975. After fifteen years of fighting, war and famine had killed a third of the population. Few heard of the war because Indonesia sealed its borders, barring all foreigners and reporters from entry. Life was so closely controlled that villagers had to answer twice daily roll calls. Pope Paul II visited in October 1989, and only then did Indonesian officials allow admission to the foreign press in an attempt to convince the world that the fighting had ceased. The pope's greatest concern during his visit was the government's birth control program, which distributed contraceptives to the populace. The local bishop stated that no birth control was needed since so many had died.

India has been the locus of religious wars for hundreds of years, resulting in millions of deaths in the last seventy years alone. No one knows for certain but it is reliably estimated that one million people were killed in 1947 during the conflict between Hindus and Muslims that ended in the formation of the state of Pakistan; three million more were slaughtered in 1971 when Bangladesh became independent.

Violence between Muslims and Hindus continues under President Modi, who is a champion of Hindu nationalism. In 2018 Christians filed 240 complaints of harassment with the Indian police but only 25 were charged as criminal violations. Any Christian accused of proselytizing Hindus is beaten up. Several Indian states have anti-conversion laws that prohibit any attempt to convert Hindus to Christianity, or any other religion.

If religion were removed from the equation, war might eventually pass from our vocabulary. There is more at stake when the opposing sides belong to a different religion, and this is the case in literally every conflict, whether atheistic or Orthodox Christian Russia against many countries in the West, or those in the abbreviated list above.

The idea of heresy is now de-emphasized and is only incidentally contained in such as *The Catholic Word Book*. The partial excising of heresy as a concept, however, has not led to its replacement by a concept of tolerance.

Monsignor John Essef, who lived in the Levant for years, addressed this subject in *Our Sunday Visitor:*

> "In every place where Islam has become a majority—without exception—it has imposed Sharia Law and subjects non-believers to live in that Muslim state as second-class citizens. . . . To the fundamentalist Muslim, ecumenism is anathema and dialogue is weakness, indifference and a betrayal of Allah. For Islam, there is only one revelation: the final word has been spoken in the Qur'an, and Mohammed is the final prophet."

Monsignor Essef failed to mention that the fundamentalists of all religions feel ecumenism is weakness and a betrayal of their particular god and that Christian fundamentalists act the same as Muslim fundamentalists. Would it be inaccurate to say that for fundamentalist

Christians there is only one revelation—that the final word has been spoken in the Bible and Jesus Christ is the final prophet? In countries or states where Catholicism or another Christian sect is in the majority, members of other religions are second-class citizens and have little chance at political office—for example, a non-Mormon in Utah.

The Christian God of the Bible avenges the blood of his servants and renders vengeance against his adversaries (Deut. 32:43). God avenges the enemies of his children (Isa. 1:24). God avenges his own elect (Luke 18:7), and he does it speedily (Luke 18:8). The enemies of the Lord will perish (Ps. 92:9). This is the morality of the Christian religion.

> "Appoint a wicked man against him; let an accuser bring him to trial. When he is tried, let him come forth guilty; let his prayer be counted as sin! May his days be few; may another seize his goods! May his children be fatherless, and his wife a widow! May his children wander about and beg; May they be driven out of the ruins they inhabit! May the creditor

seize all that he has; may strangers plunder the fruits of his toil! Let there be none to extend kindness to him, nor any to pity his fatherless children! May his posterity be cut off; may his name be blotted out in the second generation! May the iniquity of his fathers be remembered before the LORD, and let not the sin of his mother be blotted out! Let them be before the LORD continually; and may his memory be cut off from the earth."

109th Psalm

In most religions the final word is that of their god. The gods of all other religions are heretical, whether the word *heresy* is deemphasized or expressly used.

In his book *East to West: A Journey Around the World* (1958), Arnold Toynbee sums up the inability of governments and religions to live in peace:

"In one respect the 'higher' religions have

brought calamity on the World and discredit on themselves: they have seldom been content to live and let live, side by side; and their attempts to eliminate one another have been responsible for many of the bitterest conflicts and cruelest atrocities that have ever disgraced our history. In this, the two world religions of Jewish origin, Christianity and Islam, have been the worst offenders; but Hinduism, and even Buddhism, have not been guiltless."

Buddhists have recently honed religious animosities in Sri Lanka and Myanmar. During twenty-five years of civil war in Sri Lanka, Buddhist monks urged a holy war against the Tamil Tigers, who are Hindu, Christian, and Muslim. The monks opposed negotiations with or concessions to Tamil minorities; their goal was complete destruction. Buddhists supported a purely military solution to the conflict that erupted in 2009 after ethnic riots in 1956, 1958, 1977, 1981 and 1983, on the theory that Sri Lanka is a Buddhist promised land and that Tamils do not belong there, though the Tamils have lived on the island since the second century B.C.E. Christian missionaries were described by the Buddhist hierarchy as terrorists. In Myanmar the Buddhist government and military slaughtered Rohingyas (Muslims) by the thousands, beginning in August of 2017, forcing approximately half a million into exile in Bangladesh. In March 2018 the Sri Lankan government declared a state of emergency to stop communal clashes between majority Buddhists and minority Muslims, who accused the majority of genocide.

When an individual's "immortal soul" depends on the veracity of one's religion, all other religions are necessarily considered heretical. The concept of the heretic was invented by those who said love your neighbor and turn the other cheek. The foundation for the concept of heresy is a belief in intellectual slavery—if someone believes differently, ostracize or kill him. On the basis of this concept Christians killed Christians by the millions for eight hundred years.

The Crusades and the
Inquisitions

No organization can survive if its basic tenets are successfully challenged. Disagreement with a religious tenet is a challenge to the religion's validity and its very existence. If one tenet were to change, that would imply that others may similarly be subject to change, which means the tenets are fallible, possibly signaling the end of the religion.

There have been no greater atrocities in the history of the world than those committed in the name of religion, and no religion is exempt from this truth. Catholics burned Lutherans, and Lutherans burned Episcopalians, who burned Presbyterians, and vice versa, over generations. To this day no heretic, with the exception of Joan of Arc, has been forgiven by any church. Tolerance is mentioned nowhere in the Bible.

The two primary atrocities of the Christian churches spanned hundreds of years and are known generically as the Crusades and the Inquisitions. These two innocent-sounding and even patriotic terms hide a history of horror. Were we ever told in school how many millions perished in the Crusades and for what purpose other than to glorify the Christian religion? There were seven principal Crusades and many expeditions to drive the Muslims from the Holy Land, to free it from the "infidels," and capture Jerusalem.

The First Crusade was ordered by Pope Urban II on November 28, 1095. It drew six million people over several years, or about 10 percent of the population of Europe. The drawing card to drop everything and go fight the infidels was the forgiveness of all sins and a guaranteed entry into heaven—the archetypal Holy War. Out of six million people who participated in several waves, twenty thousand reached Jerusalem, massacring the inhabitants, young and old, women and children. An eyewitness description stated, "In Solomon's Porch and in his Temple, our men rode in the blood of the Saracens up to the knees of their horses."

The seed for the Crusades was planted when the Persians seized the True Cross in their 614 C.E. capture of Jerusalem, massacring 65,000 Christians and selling 35,000 survivors into slavery. Jerusalem was retaken by Emperor Heraclius in 630 C.E. but surrendered to Caliph Omar in 638. By 717 the Muslim empire had spread to North Africa, Spain, Persia, and India. The Muslims tolerated those who worshiped one god, such as Christians and Jews (though Christians and Jews were second-class citizens in Muslim countries); others were killed or converted to Islam. The Catholic church required pilgrimages to Jerusalem for penance, which were allowed by Muslim authorities.

The First Crusade officially began on August 15, 1096, but peasants led by Peter the Hermit were anxious to begin and left nine months earlier, soon after the pope's November order, arriving in Constantinople in July 1096. Of Peter the Hermit's fifteen thousand followers, three thousand survived their crossing into Asia Minor, escaping back to Europe by ship.

The second wave of peasants left Europe in mid-1096, slaughtering Jews found on the way and confiscating their possessions. The second wave was turned back at the Hungarian border; by autumn it had been defeated. The third wave consisted of the great lords and noblemen who set out in late 1096, well-armed and with one hundred thousand men, prepared to live off the land, which meant living off the people they passed on the way. Most had sold their possessions, intending to settle in the newly conquered Holy Land. The booty of battle became so lucrative, however, that four hundred miles from Jerusalem, after taking Antioch, the nobles began to settle in. Their men threatened mutiny and insisted on continuing. On July 14, 1099, after three years of battle, starvation, and disease, the First Crusade—the only successful one—reached Jerusalem and conquered it; only twenty-three hundred men survived. All Jews were slaughtered and infidels expelled. The Muslims immediately reconquered the lands between Jerusalem and Constantinople, however, closing the previously protected route to Jerusalem.

The Crusades lasted two hundred years, killing

millions of Jews, Christians, Muslims, and the unaffiliated. There has been bad blood between Christians and Muslims ever since. The heroes and leaders of the Crusades, the Knights Templar, were suppressed by the Catholic church upon their return to Europe in 1309 and were tortured to confess heresy. Because the knights were populist figures, they represented a rival to the power of the church. Accordingly, their goods were confiscated, and they were left paupers. Philip the Fair burned fifty-four Knights Templar in Paris on May 12, 1310.

* * *

By the 1100s, the church controlled all of Europe. Kings, princes, and armies were subservient to a priest and ranked far below bishops and the pope. With no legitimate authority in Europe outside the Catholic church, dissent threatened the fabric of society. By the eleventh century, dissent was treated as a combination of heresy and treason.

The Inquisitions evolved in Italy, France, and Germany, spreading to Spain in a far different form in the late fifteenth century, and then to possessions of Spain, including Mexico in the New World. Instead of a centralized all-powerful tribunal wreaking havoc on nondevout Catholics, there were many separate Inquisitions, established with various motives in different time periods and in many countries.

To understand the various Inquisitions requires a

background in the history of the Roman Catholic church: absolute power corrupting absolutely. The lowest priest was believed to have supernatural powers; his person and possessions were inviolate. Because the priest was above the law, his crimes were not subject to secular authority, which was in all events subservient to the church. The only discipline against a priest came directly from Rome, and there was no discipline in Rome. The means to political power was through the priesthood, which, with few exceptions, attracted the unscrupulous. (Religious affiliation remains a sine qua non of political power in most countries of the world, including the United States.)

The traditional Christian values of humility, charity, and self-abnegation went missing from the Catholic church and its clergy in the Middle Ages. The Christian flock was viewed as sheep to be shorn (compare Protestant televangelists today), and the priests were expert shearers. Bribery ruled. For example, the archbishop of Tours lifted excommunication from King Philip I in exchange for Philip's appointing the archbishop's male courtesan, Flora, to head the See of Orleans. Popes lived with concubines, female "relatives," nuns, and the daughters of priests. Priests bled the people dry in order to raise the exactions required by the pope. The pope sold letters allowing any bearer to excommunicate whomever the bearer wished. Excommunication meant banishment from Europe. Pay or leave. These letters were often forged, as was the papal seal; bishops sold their own letters, and many priests kept concubines. By 1397, during the age of Chaucer, eighty priests in the Hereford Diocese were accused of keeping one or more concubines. Divorces were sold; marriages required large bribes to absolve the parties from violating taboos against possible consanguinity in remote past generations. Priests made regular gifts to boys aged seven to fourteen—shades of the twenty-first century—and awarded churches to some youngsters. Tithes were enforced against the poorest of the poor, who received nothing in return, except a guarantee that their immortal souls would go directly to purgatory and eventually to heaven. Competing jurisdictions within the church collected tithes many times over from the same parishioners. There were fines for every conceivable sin, and confession was required of everyone. Communion was unavailable until all fines and exactions had been paid. The church diplomatically suggested to the dying and their families that only if the estate were willed to the church could the church be expected to pray for the soul in purgatory so it could get to heaven. The church settled for a law passing a third of all estates to it. Many nunneries were houses of prostitution. Criminals joined abbeys to escape prosecution. Many churches became wine bars featuring jugglers, actors, gamblers, and whores. The church owned Europe and was absolutely corrupt.

Some church leaders tried to stem the tide of corruption, but with little effect. Scattered abbeys fed the poor during famines, especially the famine of 1197. Several bishops tried over and over for reform. Pope Alexander III denounced the sale of dispensations, limiting their effectiveness to one year, which brought in even more revenue upon renewal. Much of the dispensation system was implemented to compete with the Muslims, who promised eternal bliss and concubines for those who died as martyrs. The church promised the same to participants in the Crusades, without the concubines. Before the end of the Crusades in 1291, far greater dispensations were required to obtain soldiers. Dispensations from all sin (guaranteed entry to heaven without passing purgatory) were granted to those who would pay for others to go on a Crusade in their place. Dispensations were also given for sins of fathers and mothers. The priests liberally applied their levers: the Eucharist (the communion wafer), holy relics, holy water, exorcism, and prayer. Anything could be had for a price.

Even uneducated peasants began to suspect that something was wrong. The most difficult heresy for the church was the accusation that the sacraments were polluted by sinful priests. In 1074 Gregory VII declared that no one should attend the mass of a priest who had a concubine, but this was neither enforced nor enforceable. Instead of purifying the churches, this order emptied them.

The first heretics were burned at Orleans in 1017. The rebellion grew, and other leaders arose: Henry, Monk of Lausanne; Arnold of Brescia (burned in 1155); and Peter Waldo of Lyon. These heretics relied on biblical texts and were far more learned in the Bible than most priests, bishops, or even the pope. They gave away their earthly goods, seeking to contrast their own behavior with that of priests, who sold penances and dispensations. They had many followers who were disgusted with the corruption of the church, and they constituted a real threat.

The Catholic church considered the Bible too profound for common people, only modifying this position in 1965 with the Second Vatican Council. The Council of Beziers in 1233–34 forbade possession of the Bible in Latin. Any person failing to turn in his Bible was deemed a heretic. The authority of today's priests is based on the ability to interpret the "seemingly" contradictory provisions of the Bible. Yet priests in the Middle Ages were ignorant of the Bible, whereas heretics knew it backward and forward. Because the heretics were more skillful with the Bible than the inquisitors, they were not allowed to argue theology upon pain of death, which they were awarded in any event.

Heretics, such as the Waldesians, reproached the church for its wealth, feudal privilege, sinful priests, sex without reproduction, and any portion of the Catholic dogma not supported directly by the Bible, which left little. They heretically held that it was better to feed the poor than to adorn church walls, arguing that Christ had no miter, sable, or bejeweled chalice. They said the inquisitorial courts were not for justice but for the monetary gain of the church.

Alonso II of Aragon decreed in 1194 that heresies and heretics were public enemies, and listening to them was treason to the church, requiring confiscation of the listeners' goods. Any injury inflicted on a heretic brought the favor of royalty. Alonso's son, Pedro II, added burning at the stake as the appropriate penalty for listening to heresy. In these early days foretelling the formal Inquisitions, the populace would drag heretics out of prison to burn them; they did so in Soissons in 1141, Liege in 1144, and Cologne in 1151. The church initially protested that vigilante justice was too harsh. Still, the rebellion spread, and the church began to see the wisdom of its followers. The rebels were simple men, detesting the corrupt priesthood. Their main offense was their zeal in making converts and their great success. Many memorized the whole Bible, or at least the New Testament. The persecuted felt themselves to be the only true Catholics. By 1167, the Cathari ("pure" with no sex or possessions) set up a parallel church in southern France. Death for heresy was officially proclaimed in 1209.

On orders of the church in July 1209, the Cathari headquarters at Beziers, France, was stormed by recently returned Crusaders, who slaughtered twenty thousand men, women, and children in three hours. The preferred method of killing heretics, other than by fire, was to first mutilate them by cutting off the nose, then tearing out the eyes and tongue.

Innocent III pursued and exterminated the Albigensians (Cathars) during the 1200s, serving to further consolidate the House of Capet and the Kingdom of France. At the 1215 Lateran Council, he ordered the faithful to report all heretics for extermination. He believed that the fall of Jerusalem in 1187 signaled the 666 years of the beast of the Apocalypse, evidenced by the swarming spread of Islam. The purpose of the council, attended by bishops, abbots, and representatives of most secular rulers, was to reform the church, reconquer Jerusalem, and suppress heresy. The council ordained the Fifth Crusade for June 1, 1217, and prescribed various penalties for heresy, including the usual ones of confiscation, removal from public office, and excommunication, plus punishment by the secular arm, which meant death. Also required were expulsion from lands, the reporting of other heretics, and the removal of any bishop failing to follow these rules. By 1325 the "pure" Cathars were completely exterminated.

The Catholic Word Book justifies the Inquisition[s] by saying, "The Inquisition was a creature of its time when crimes against the faith, which threatened the good of the Christian community, were regarded also as crimes against the state, and when heretical doctrines of such extremists as the Cathari and Albigensians threatened the very fabric of society."

* * *

In 1233 Gregory IX entrusted the Inquisition to the Dominicans, and this began its organized phase. Gregory set the stage in 1231, requiring excommunication of all Cathars, Waldensians, heretics, their followers and friends, and those failing to denounce known heretics. The document also prohibited representation by an attorney, excluded the children of heretics from the church, and required the demolition of the home of any heretic. Acquittals were almost unknown. The Inquisition excommunicated any civil magistrate who refused to burn a heretic. Perjurers and heretics were allowed to testify against any accused. The testimony of two people was required for a conviction of heresy, but the testimony of only one was sufficient to justify torture, and torture usually resulted in a confession, removing the necessity for a second witness. Favorable witnesses were unavailable because they were labeled heretics if they testified in support of an accused heretic.

Heresy was treason because there was no separation of church and state, and an accusation of treason allowed the confiscation of the accused's property. There was no need to wait until conviction to take the accused's property because the verdict was known in advance. Since an accusation of heresy, even against the dead, resulted in confiscation of all property, trials of the dead became very lucrative and resulted in complete estates passing to the church and the impoverishment of the accused's heirs. A popular proverb in the 1200s was "Justice is a very profitable job." The church sold offices allowing their purchasers to try people for heresy. The only way to escape an accusation of heresy was by bribery, which was difficult because all the possessions of the accused had already been confiscated. Often the accused would face preliminary questioning. At this stage fines, mitigations, and dispensations were both available and rampant.

(A similar situation exists today with regard to the confiscation of property, no matter by whom owned, if drugs are found in or on that property in the United States of America. However, in February 2019 the U.S. Supreme Court, in a unanimous decision, struck down unlimited forfeitures, requiring the value of property forfeited to be proportional to the offense—whatever that means—in a case where the defendant sold heroin valued at $225 to undercover police, resulting in the forfeiture of his $52,000 Land Rover. In 2018 the small town of Surprise, Arizona, received $550,000 in forfeited property, similar to police departments around the country.)

The combination of the Crusades and the various Inquisitions impoverished the entire population of Europe, except those connected to the church and its subordinate secular authorities. The various Inquisitions (Roman Catholic, Protestant, and Spanish) lasted more than eight hundred years, from 1017 to the 1800s.

The best-known inquisitor before the Spanish Inquisition was Bernard Gui. The following is the 1321 account of his trial of the Waldesian heretic Hugh of Vienne:

> "He refused to swear, pretending the feigned reason that he dared not, because, having sworn on another occasion, he had incurred the falling sickness. . . . Therefore, we, Bishop of Pamiers, intimated and explained to him the written law, that any man suspected in matters of faith, and brought before the judge, and required to swear as to the truth, must be judged a heretic if he refuse to swear; yet he would on no account swear; nay, he said that it repented him to have sworn elsewhere before the

said bishop and the Inquisitor of Carcassonne, saying that he had thus sinned grievously and believed that it would be a sin to swear again; nor, though oftentimes required, would he thenceforth swear to tell the truth in a case of faith. . . . Item, he said that man sinneth who compelled another to swear, for the Lord hath commanded us not to swear. Item, that he believed his soul would be saved if he were judged to death for the said cause [of refusing to swear]. Item, asked whether the secular powers can without sin condemn to death men guilty of mortal crimes, as homicides and other felons, he answered that he knew not what to believe in this matter, for the Lord commanded Thou shalt not kill. Item, he said and affirmed that he would persist and live and die in the aforesaid faith, though often questioned [on that point]; nor would he swear in any manner. Item, he said and affirmed that he would not believe or obey the Lord Pope, if he told him it is lawful to swear to the truth, and that purgatory existed, and that the prayers of the Church availed dead men. Item, that he did not believe himself subject to the Lord Pope, but to God alone. Afterwards it was said and expounded to him that, unless he revoked and abandoned these errors, he would be proceeded against as an impenitent and obstinate heretic; yet he answered that he would stand by them in life and death; nor would he in any way abandon them; to wit, that swearing is sinful, for the truth or for other causes; that there is no purgatory after this life; that prayers for the dead avail them not; that excommunication, however rightly and canonically pronounced, did not shut him out from the Kingdom of God or from spiritual benefits; and that the secular powers which possess jurisdiction, sin when they slay malefactors: also, that he held himself not subject to the Pontiff of Rome except when he commandeth the same as God doth."

Waldesians persisted for centuries in out-of-the-way places and exist today, though their principles have been absorbed by mainstream Protestants or are now considered trivial. On a single day in 1393 the Inquisition burned 150 Waldesians at Grenoble; Waldesians were slaughtered en masse by the church in 1488 and 1686.

An inquisition was commenced by either a special individual summons or a general summons to the population in the area. When an individual was accused, he was first told by his priest, who announced the name from the pulpit for three consecutive Sundays, after which the accused was expected to, and usually did, turn himself in to the nearest secular prison to await trial. Those failing to turn themselves in were automatically excommunicated and become outcasts. A general inquisition began with a sermon, after which heretics who confessed were absolved from excommunication. But confession by itself was insufficient to obtain absolution. The accused was also required to implicate at least one other person as a heretic, otherwise he was sentenced to life in prison or burned at the stake. Because accused were required to implicate others the number of accused snowballed, and much of the community would become accused of heresy. One woman in 1254 implicated 169 other "heretics."

When torture was officially authorized in 1256, the Inquisition honed barbarity to its finest point. The tools of the Inquisition were ingenious devices. The six most used tortures were: (1) Ordeal of water. The accused was forced to swallow between five and ten liters of water until confession was obtained. We know today that ingesting that amount of water causes the brain to swell and results in death, similar to waterboarding in Iraq. (2) Ordeal of fire. The accused's feet were caked with animal fat and placed into a roaring fire until confession; the feet were literally fried. (3) The pulley (also known as the strappado). The arms were tied behind the back, and the accused was hoisted by his wrists to the ceiling and then dropped, pulling his arms from their sockets. This was repeated until a confession was obtained. (4) The wheel. The accused was strapped to a large wheel and his body beaten with hammers, bars, and clubs until confession or death. (5) Stivaletto or brodequins. The accused's legs were strapped to boards and wedges were driven between the board and legs until the pressure crushed or splintered the leg or confession was obtained. (6) The rack. The body was stretched until pulled apart or until confession. The Torture Museum in Ghent, Belgium, displays these interesting items.

Because of Catholic and reformed Protestant religiosity, people were slaughtered for thinking the following: that there was one God or there was a Trinity of Gods/God; that the Holy Ghost was younger than God or God was older than Christ; that good works saved a man without faith or faith was sufficient without good works; that a baby was not burned eternally for failing to have his head sprinkled by a priest; or that three entities added together made more than one. People could also be executed for speaking of God as having a nose, saying God is an essence, or denying God used his finger as a pen; for denying that Christ was his own father; for believing in purgatory or not believing in purgatory; for pretending priests can forgive sins or denying such power; for denying witches ride through the air on sticks; for saying the Virgin Mary was born like other people; for saying a man's rib is not large enough to make a regular-sized woman; for saying all prayers are answered, or that none are; for denying that diseases (such as AIDS) are sent to punish unbelief or sin; for denying the absolute authority of the Bible; for possessing a Bible; for attending mass or refusing to attend mass; for carrying a cross or refusing to carry a cross; or for being a Catholic, a Protestant, an Episcopalian, a Presbyterian, a Baptist, or a Quaker. Every virtue has been a crime, and every crime a virtue.

A curious chapter in the Inquisitions involved the rivalry between two Franciscan sects, resulting in the excommunication of the splinter Fraticelli sect by John XXII on December 30, 1317, which followed vows of poverty in imitation of Saint Francis of Assisi. Because of the fear of extremist movements, poverty was condemned in 1323 and, according to the 1638 Vatican manuscript *Codice Urbinate,* over fifteen thousand Fraticelli were executed. The distinctions between saint and heretic were exceedingly faint.

The intensity of the Inquisitions varied by time and place. Venice was independent, so its inquisitors grew rich, not having to share confiscations with the church or the state. Few punishments other than confiscation were imposed. The Inquisition was so corrupt (meaning the church failed to receive its share) in Venice that Boniface VIII suspended it in 1302.

The Aztecs of Mexico were conquered in 1521, and the Spanish Inquisition of Mexico began in 1522. The beginnings of the Mexican Inquisition were largely political, directed against Cortés and his followers. When Cortés went to Honduras in 1524, he left his cousin Rodrigo de Paz in charge. The Inquisition imprisoned de Paz and tortured him, roasting his feet until his toes fell off, and then burning his feet to the ankles in an attempt to find out where Cortés had hidden his "bragged-about" gold.

In the Mexican Inquisition's first ten years only one person was exonerated. Doctors were targeted because the church resented their interference with its role in healing. Many were accused of being Lutherans. Indians were persecuted for continuing to venerate their traditional gods. Dominicans and Franciscans tried each other for heresy on the basis of differences in scriptural interpretation, such as whether a church member receives grace from the sacraments or is already in a state of grace upon conversion. A formal edict against the Jews was issued in 1523. The first burnings for heresy in Mexico occurred on October 17, 1528. From 1572 through 1601 over a thousand trials were held, with accusations against Jews and Protestants, especially Lutherans and Germans suspected of being Lutheran. Some heretics were sold as slaves. Hundreds of volumes of sixteenth-century manuscripts detail the Mexican Inquisition.

The Mexican Inquisition coincided with inquisitions in Peru, Guatemala, the Philippines, and other Catholic countries. The Inquisition lasted in Sicily from 1487 to 1782. It was also waged in Sardinia, the Canary Islands, Portugal, and all of South America.

The Inquisition in Spain was a marginal improvement over the wholesale slaughter of the Jews. In Spain, as in France and Italy centuries earlier, the Catholic church was corrupt. Most priests kept concubines and the courts were run by bribery. Ferdinand and Isabella united Spain, driving out the Moors and destroying the castles of forty-two robber barons, making Spain the most modern country in Europe and its most efficient totalitarian state. Ferdinand considered the Conversos, "converted" Jews, to be his biggest problem. They filled his court and ran much of the country. (Lest Anglo-Saxons become smug, Edward I expelled all Jews from England.)

The Spanish Inquisition was established in 1478 by order of Sixtus IV, though controlled by the crown, which appointed the inquisitors and kept all confiscations. The inquisitors kept concubines and took bribes, which horrified Sixtus IV, who ordered fair trials henceforth and stated that the Inquisition in Spain was motivated by confiscations. His order was issued in response to a bribe by Conversos and was never enforced because Ferdinand ignored it.

By 1560 a witness could be bought to testify to anything. Inquisitor Lucero kept a permanent witness handy for use against anyone he wished to destroy. Bought witnesses were allowed to appear as different persons during the same trial. Jews offered ransoms to Ferdinand, but Isabella refused their acceptance. On March 20, 1492, all Jews were ordered to leave Spain by July 31, under pain of death. The order was not published in Barcelona until May 1, however, so Jews there had three months to settle their affairs, sell their nonportable possessions, and leave. Those who failed to meet the deadline had all their goods confiscated and were killed. Those fleeing were able to keep few possessions, and many were robbed and murdered in Spanish seaports and in other countries upon their arrival. About fifty thousand Jews theoretically converted to Christianity and stayed in Spain.

The Spanish fetish for a pure Spain and pure blood resulted in a similar order against the Moors in 1609. The Moors were given three days to leave the country. Their goods were forfeited, they were robbed of what they tried to carry out of the country, and women and children were sold as slaves. The engineer of the expulsion of the Moors, Archbishop Ribera, was beatified by the church. Catholics may now pray to God in his name.

By 1786 the Spanish Inquisition was comparatively

dormant, though it still pulled people from their beds in the middle of the night and employed torture, and most priests lived with women. The last inquisitorial execution occurred in 1834 in Spain, and the Spanish Inquisition officially ended in 1869. No one knows how many were condemned to death by the Inquisition in its eight-hundred-year history, from the first execution in 1017 to the last in 1834—the archives of the Catholic church remain sealed in Rome—but estimates range into the tens of millions.

The Catholic Word Book explains the Catholic archives: "The strictest secrecy is always in effect for confidential records concerning matters of conscience, and documents of this kind are destroyed as soon as circumstances permit." The church responded to the cruelty of the Inquisition by canonizing the worst of its inquisitors, Pope Pius V, in 1712.

In December 1990, the Vatican proposed beatifying Queen Isabella I of Spain as the first step in her elevation to sainthood, in time for the five hundredth anniversary of Columbus's discovery of America, which brought Christianity to the New World. The move outraged Jews and Muslims. The head of the Federation of Spanish Jewish Communities called Isabella "a symbol of intolerance," pointing out that her canonization "would reopen old wounds that we thought were closed forever." Jewish representatives in Spain, Italy, and Britain asked the Vatican to shelve the petition for beatification. The chairman of the Islamic Society for the Promotion of Religious Tolerance was quoted in the *London Times* as saying, "Muslims and Jews were forced at the point of a sword to convert to Christianity or die. She is more a demon than a saint." The postulator arguing Isabella's case before the Vatican called her "one of the great women of history" and "one of the great Christians of history," though he admits to being hard-pressed to find a miracle attributable to Isabella. (Two miracles are needed for beatification.) The beatification process was shelved in 1999 and again in 2003 but was reinstituted in 2018 by the unanimous vote of the bishops of Grenada. Queen Isabella may one day be a saint.

Pius X dropped the term "Inquisition" from the official title of the Inquisition in 1908, and it was henceforth known as the Holy Office. In 1965 Pope Paul VI renamed it the Sacred Congregation for the Doctrine of the Faith, which it remains in 2018, though the word "sacred" has been excised.

* * *

Religious toleration is a recent concept. The toleration by any religion of another religion (or the nonreligious) increases in direct proportion to the religion's inability to do anything about heresy. When the Catholic church exercised absolute power, heresy meant confiscation of all property, exile, imprisonment, torture, and death.

When Henry VIII established the Episcopal church, he

instructed Parliament to pass "an Act for abolishing of diversity of opinion":

> "First, that in the sacrament was the real body and blood of Jesus Christ. Second, that the body and blood of Jesus Christ was in the bread, and the blood and body of Jesus Christ was in the wine. Third, that priests should not marry. Fourth, that vows of chastity are of perpetual obligation. Fifth, that private masses are to be continued; and, Sixth, that auricular confessions to a priest must be maintained."

The punishment for denying the first article was death. Denial of the others required imprisonment. Two denials required death. (None of these articles are part of the Episcopal dogma today.)

The American colonies enacted many similar laws; the following passage is from a law in force in colonial Maryland:

"That is any person shall hereafter, within this province, wittingly, maliciously, and advisedly, by writing or speaking, blaspheme or curse God, or deny our savior, Jesus Christ, to be the Son of God, or shall deny the Holy Trinity, the Father, Son, and Holy Ghost, or the Godhead of any of the three persons [sic], or the unity of the Godhead, or shall utter any profane words concerning the Holy Trinity, or any of the persons [sic] thereof, and shall be convicted by verdict, shall, for the first offence, be bored through the tongue, and fined twenty pounds to be levied of his body. And for the second offence, the offender shall be stigmatized by burning in the forehead with the letter B, and fined forty pounds. And that for the third offence the offender shall suffer death without the benefit of the clergy."

Gore Vidal put the American founding in perspective in an *Elle* interview:

"Actually, the Puritans had been driven out of England because no one could stand them. They went to Holland where they proceeded to persecute the Dutch, who eventually drove them out. Our history books say they were driven out because of persecution—yet they were persecuting the Dutch who put them on boats and headed them west."

Every Christian has a duty to kill the enemies of God, and if anyone hints there's another God, Christians are duty bound to kill the bearer of the suggestion, whether the person is his father, mother, relative, friend, or wife (Deut. 13:6–11). God's children read the Bible and understood the words differently, and slaughter resulted. Millions of good people are Christians. They are hardworking and self-sacrificing. Many believe, however, that disagreement with the Bible is a mortal crime and that disbelievers are eternally damned, and know that the Bible orders unbelievers slain.

The plain fact is that tolerating the believers of another god is treason to the religion's one true god. How can a believer be true to his god if he tolerates other gods, when by the infallible principles of his religion there's only one god, which is the god of his religion?

Christians, Muslims, and Jews

The history of anti-Semitism is a history of Christianity. Christians celebrated the destruction of the Jewish Temple in 70 C.E. as punishment by the Christian God for Jewish rejection of Jesus Christ. Even before the advent of Christianity, however, Romans and Greeks spread stories that Jews were lepers driven from Egypt and that they practiced ritual murder of Greeks. Because the Jews held to only one god, rejecting the multiple Greek and Roman gods, and stayed by themselves in close-knit communities, they were considered suspicious and ostracized. Evolutionary psychologist John Pearce identifies a logical and natural reason for anti-Semitism:

> "In the hunting-and-gathering stage of human development, for which we are all still wired biologically, other people, strangers, were the most dangerous creatures one was likely to encounter. You were far more likely to get yourself killed by an outsider to your clan than by a natural disaster or an animal.

To fear strangers is just as
natural, just as fundamentally
human, as to love your own
family."

Our continuing psychological division into groups,
whether religious, political, economic, racial, sexual, or any
other, serves to further solidify the us-against--them
syndrome, encouraging strife among the members of a single
species.

The first wholesale slaughter of Jews occurred in
Alexandria in 38 C.E. Men, women, and children were
dragged through the streets, beaten to death, and burned on
bonfires after they were declared intruders for ridiculing
Herod Agrippa, a representative of the Roman emperor.

In *Peri Pascha*, the second-century homily of Melito
of Sardis, the Christian bishop accused the Jews of
murdering God:

"Even Pilate washed his
hands, you killed him on the
great Holy Day (Jewish
Passover). You killed the
Lord in the middle of
Jerusalem. . . . He who created
the universe was himself
nailed to the wood. The Lord

was killed. God was murdered. The King of Israel was eliminated by Jewish hands. Oh, this unheard-of murder! Oh, this unheard-of injustice!"

Though it may be difficult to understand how God could be murdered, Matthew 27:25 says the Jews confessed, "then answered all the people and said, His blood be on us, and on our children." Relative tolerance ended in 313 C.E., when Christianity became the official religion of the Roman Empire. The Jews were excluded from entering Jerusalem except one day a year; violation resulted in death.

Augustine called Jews degraded and fit only to be slaves to the church. The laws formulated between 213 and 437 C.E. were codified into the Theodosian Code in 438 and contained two chapters of anti-Jewish laws, Jews being described as a depraved sect, a criminal religion, and an infectious disease. The Justinian Code of 534, which is the basis for European and American law, relegated Jews to second-class citizenship, imposed the death sentence for anyone tempting a Christian to convert to Judaism, forbade sex between Jews and Christians, prescribed banishment and loss of all possessions for circumcising a Christian, excluded Jews from public office, and required death and confiscation of all possessions for anyone building a new synagogue.

Mohammed saw Islam as perfecting Christianity and Judaism but declared holy war on all nonbelievers, particularly Jews. The male Jews in Medina were slaughtered, the women and children deported. The Quran provides: "Thou wilt surely find that the strongest in enmity against those who believe are the Jews and the idolaters" (Surah V:85). Beginning in 807 C.E. Jews in Muslim countries were required to wear yellow badges and live separately. In some places they were required to shave their heads and wear lead or iron seals around their necks. According to Islamic tradition, "A Jew will not be found alone with a Muslim without planning to kill him."

Pope Stephen III objected that Charlemagne and his successors, the Carolingians, gave equal rights to Jews. He wrote to the bishop at Narbonne:

> "Overwhelmed by concern and alarm, we received your message that the Jewish people, who remained unruly towards God and averse to our customs, have been given the same status as Christians on Christian ground. . . .

Christians work the Jewish
vineyards and fields.
Christian men and women
live with these traitors under
one roof and defile their souls
with blasphemous words day
and night; these unfortunate
wretches must humble
themselves to those dogs
every day, every hour, and
accede to their every whim.
Justice alone demands that the
promises made to these
traitors be declared invalid, so
that the death of the crucified
savior will finally be
avenged."

The First Crusade began with the slaughter of
thousands of Jews along the Rhine. The property of dead
Jews was used to support the Crusades. Muslims murdered
six thousand Jews in the Moroccan city of Fez in 1037 and
in 1066 killed over five thousand in Granada, Spain. The
Muslims gave the Jews the choice of death or conversion,
the same choice Spanish Christians later offered to Jews.
Beginning in 1215 with the Fourth Lateran Council, which

declared the communion wafer to be the actual body of Christ, Jews were required by the pope and his bishops to wear round yellow badges in France and pointed hats in Germany. The stated purpose was to prevent Christians, out of ignorance of identity, from having sex with Jews.

On June 19, 1239, Pope Gregory IX ordered confiscation of all copies of the Talmud. French Dominicans carried out this order on the first Sabbath in Lent by raiding the synagogues and removing all Hebrew literature. All the Jewish literature in Paris was burned on a central bonfire in 1242. Pope John XXII reiterated the order that all copies of the Talmud be burned in 1322, on the eve of the Jewish Passover.

In the Middle Ages anti-Semitism took the form of legends that the Jews ritually murdered Christian children to obtain blood to mix with their unleavened bread during Passover, to add potency to their wine, or to remove the "stink of Jews." (Since the Jews were associated with the devil, they were believed to share his characteristics, notably his smell of sulfur.) When a child was not easily available, the Jews were reputed to steal a host (the communion wafer representing the body of Christ) and to burn or puncture it to obtain the fresh blood of Christ, thus ritually crucifying him again. The Catholic church certified many miracles where the host was rescued from Jews who were later burned at the stake.

126

Jews were accused of poisoning wells and causing the plague. These accusations in Switzerland and Germany resulted in Jews being tortured on the rack, beheaded, and burned at the stake. Sixty large Jewish communities and 150 smaller ones were razed and all occupants slaughtered. After all Jews were killed in Zwolle, Switzerland, in 1349, the burgomaster stated, "They have been killed for the love of God with fire and the sword." A German newspaper, however, wrote that the Jews were killed to obtain their possessions: "Their jingling coins formed the poison that killed the Jews"—and financed the expedition to discover the Americas. During the Middle Ages, Jews and their possessions were considered the property of the sovereign.

In 1412 the Laws of Valladolid required Jews to live in enclosed areas, to continue wearing badges, and to grow beards. Jewish doctors were prohibited from treating Christians. Pope Sixtus IV issued a papal bull in 1478 allowing Ferdinand and Isabella to establish a special Inquisition against baptized Jews, which had been sought by Spanish bishops for decades. This Inquisition was compared to the Last Judgment; the church was only doing what awaited Jews in hell. Jews had previously been required to be either baptized or burned at the stake. Most continued to follow Jewish doctrine in private, hence the Christian solution to purify the blood by burning or banishing all Jews. Popes Alexander VI, Leo X, Clement VII, and Paul III approved of the "purity of the blood" statutes, the infamous Limpieza de Sangre. Baptized Jews were called Marranos (swine), and thousands were burned at the stake until 1492, when Ferdinand and Isabella banished all Jews on a few days' notice, requiring 150,000 to flee the country with few possessions, leaving most of their wealth for Ferdinand, Isabella, and the church. By the 1600s the Jews were depicted as eternally wandering the earth without a country. Banishments were justified by Jesus' example in the Bible of driving the Jewish moneychangers from the temple.

Martin Luther originally sided with Jews in their opposition to forced membership in the Catholic church, but when the Jews refused to convert to Protestantism in 1543, he published a violently anti-Semitic tract titled *On Jews and Their Lies:*

> "What must we do with this cursed and vile race of Jews? . . . In the first place, their synagogues should be burned down and what does not burn must be covered with mud. This must be done for the honor of God and Christianity so God may see that we are Christians and we

have not simply tolerated or approved that His Son and His Christians have been subjected to lies, curses and slander. In the second place, their houses should be pulled down and destroyed. They must be housed in stables like gypsies. . . . Third, their books should be taken from them. Fourth, rabbis should be forbidden to give any more lessons on pain of death. Fifth, they should not be allowed to move around freely. Let them stay home. Sixth, they should no longer be allowed to charge interest. The money that is taken from them should be spent to help Jews who agree to be baptized."

Pope Julius III celebrated the Jewish New Year in Rome on September 9, 1553, by publicly burning all books owned or written by Jews. He ordered all Jewish books burned throughout the empire. The order was reissued by

Pope Paul IV in 1559, who had on July 12, 1555, begun confining Jews in Rome from sunset to sunrise within their ghetto, where they lived, until 1848, on a few acres of unsanitary and cramped housing. The purpose of the ghettos, besides preventing Jews from associating with Christians, was to show the world that God was continuing their punishment for murdering his son. Pope Pius V banished all Jews from Italy, except for the punishment ghettos in Rome and Ancona. Jews previously were banished from Venice (1497), Genoa (1516 and 1550), and Naples (1540).

The eighteenth-century enlightenment and the French Revolution continued the traditional treatment of the Jews. Voltaire regarded Jews as "an ignorant, barbarian people, who combine the foulest greed with a terrible superstition and an uncompromising hatred of all the peoples who tolerate them and at whose cost they enrich themselves." After the revolution, the French gave equal rights to Jews on the theory that if persecution of Jews ceased, they would give up their odious customs and religion; they would become emancipated by no longer being Jews.

Between 1848 and 1879 anti-Semitism became the basis for political parties and the election of national candidates in Germany and Austria. Because the Jews had no country, they were suspected of being traitors in their countries of residence, the most famous example being the Dreyfus affair in 1894 France.

Army captain Alfred Dreyfus was accused of passing military secrets to the Germans. He was convicted on forged evidence; his main sin was being a Jew. Dreyfus was rehabilitated only after ten years in prison and a scathing exposé and challenge to the French government by Emile Zola. During this period Jewish shops were plundered and Jews assaulted. One columnist described the Dreyfus sentencing: "Death to the Jews, cried the mob when the stripes were torn from his captain's uniform . . . when a progressive and doubtlessly highly civilized people can come to this, what can be expected of other people?"

Anti-Semitism in Russia was preserved by the Russian Orthodox Church with the argument that the Jewish presence polluted Holy Russia. Jews were segregated, taxed into poverty, granted citizenship privileges only upon conversion to Christianity, and required to give twenty-five years of military service. The crackdown on Russian Jews began in March 1881, when Alexander II was assassinated. Alexander III (1881–1894) responded to his father's assassination by oppressing the languages, cultures, and religions of non-Russians. He believed the Jews were an especially accursed people because they had "crucified the savior." By 1891, all Jews were expelled from Moscow.

In *Mein Kampf* (1924) Hitler described his attitude toward the Jews:

"And when such a tumor was carefully cut open, a little Jew was found like a maggot in rotting wood, who often blinked with eyes blinded by the sudden light. . . . what was used here to destroy all human values was a pestilence with more fatal results than those the Black Death had. Now the Jews serve as carriers of bacilli of the worst kind, and they infect souls everywhere. As is typical of all parasites, the Jew keeps enlarging his territory; he lives at the cost of his host and spreads like a dangerous bacillus."

According to his close personal friend Dietrich Eckart, Hitler was greatly influenced by Luther's writing and attitude toward Jews. Hitler appreciated the Catholic church's similar attitude, saying in 1938, "In the Gospels, the Jews cried out to Pilate, when he refused to have Jesus crucified: 'His blood be on us and our children.' Maybe I have to fulfill this curse."

On April 1, 1933, a boycott of Jewish shops and businesses began in Germany, and on April 7, all Jewish officials were fired. Hitler told two visiting Catholic bishops on April 26, 1933, "I am being attacked for the way I treat the Jews. The church has regarded the Jews as parasites for fifteen hundred years and has banished them to the ghetto. They knew what the Jews were worth. I am only continuing what has been happening the last fifteen hundred years. I may be doing Christianity the greatest of favors."

The official terror began on November 9, 1938, when hundreds of synagogues were burned, Jewish houses and shops were looted, and thirty thousand Jews were deported to camps. The ancient religious discrimination against Jews was officially reimplemented in Germany. Jews were required to wear a yellow star; the identification of a person as Jewish was supplied through the records of the Christian churches in Germany. The only objection raised by the churches was a cry for compensation for the burden of tracing Jewish genealogy.

In December 1941, the month the first permanent extermination camp was established in Chelmno, Poland, six Evangelical Church bishops and the head of the Lubeck Lutheran Church issued the following declaration:

"The regulations of the

133

'Reichspolizei' have July 7 [1941] branded the Jews as the born enemies of the people and of the Third Reich. From bitter experience centuries ago, Martin Luther advised governments to take strict measures against Jews and to banish them from German society. The Jews have opposed, misused or tampered with Christianity from the Crucifixion to the present day for their own profit. Christian baptism brings no change in the nature of a Jew, which is determined by race. Because the Evangelical Church in Germany has been ordered to give pastoral guidance to members in their religious life, it demands that Christians of the Jewish race be removed from the Evangelical Church."

Although the world did not find out for years, on January 20, 1942, in a short meeting at the villa Wannsee in Berlin, top Nazis officially adopted the Final Solution. On January 31, German execution squads reported the murder of 229,052 Jews in the Baltic countries. In that same year, Rabbi Nitra of Czechoslovakia wrote a letter to Catholic archbishop Kmetko asking for help in preventing the deportation of the Jews. The archbishop replied: "It is not a question of deportation. There [in Germany] you will not die of hunger and misery. They will murder all of you, old and young, women and children at once—it is the punishment you deserve because you murdered our Lord and Savior, Jesus Christ. There is just one possibility of escaping this fate; convert to our religion and then I shall do my best to have the order revoked."

The first selections for the gas chambers in Auschwitz-Birkenau occurred on June 23, 1942. The last gassing occurred there at the end of October 1944. Nobel Peace Prize winner Elie Wiesel asked pertinent questions:

> "In all the turmoil, this relationship [between Christians and Jews] must be reconsidered. Because a new truth struck us: when the victims were all Jews, the

murderers were all Christians. What explanation is there that a Hitler or a Himmler was never excommunicated by the Pope? That Pope Pius XII never considered it urgent, or even necessary, to condemn Auschwitz? That in the SS there was a high percentage of Christians who remained devoted to their Christian tradition until the end? That certain murderers went to confession between murders? And that all of them came from Christian families and had enjoyed a Christian upbringing? How can it be explained that being a Christian did not make their hands tremble when they shot down children, nor their consciences rebel when they drove naked and battered victims into the factories of death?"

The explanation is simple when we look at the history of religions, including Judaism. The number of religions without the taint of human blood prominent in their history can be counted on one hand and would perhaps include the Quakers and a few others. Israel treats non-Jews as second-class citizens, at best, and justifies the killing of Palestinian Muslims as self-defense.

During WWII, all countries barred Jewish immigration. Franklin Delano Roosevelt was indifferent to the problem of Jews under German rule, as were the American people and the pope. The Jewish problem under German rule was way down the priority list, especially compared to winning the war. The Jewish uprising in Palestine in 1936 had made Britons and Americans wary of Jewish claims. Because the outcome of the war was unclear until mid-1943, it wasn't until early 1944 that FDR established the War Refugee Board, probably saving about 200,000 lives; too little, too late. There is always the question of how much more could have been done, however, when the war effort was top priority. Even Jewish communities did little, because until four people escaped from Auschwitz in 1944 no one knew or believed the full extent of the horror. Palestinian Jews were divided on whether to concentrate resources on rescuing Jews or building the new state. Official U.S. policy held that the best way to help the Jews was to put all its energies into winning the war. The Allies bombed within four kilometers of Auschwitz but never bombed the railway leading there, which would have stopped deportations to the biggest death camp of all.

* * *

In 2018 Vladimir Putin suggested that Jews, among others, may have been the culprits who interfered in the 2016 U.S. election.

The same year, the Polish government passed a law criminalizing speech that would accuse Poland of complicity in the Holocaust. The criminal penalties were removed after outrage in the E.U., the U.S., and Israel.

A 2018 poll by the Pew Research Center found ample evidence of religious intolerance in European countries. Between 13 and 43 percent of respondents said they would oppose a Muslim marrying into the family (except for liberal Netherlands at 9 percent). Those who would oppose a Jew marrying into the family maxed out at 25 percent in Italy (where 43 percent would oppose a Muslim in the family, probably because Italy is bearing the brunt of the European refugee crisis from Muslim countries).

In a separate 2018 poll by the Pew Research Center, 30 percent of Polish respondents said they would not be willing to accept Jews as members of their families.

Mainline Protestant denominations, including Episcopalians, Presbyterians, and the United Church of

Christ, accept a "two-covenant" theology, which says God's covenant with the Jewish people was never abrogated and that Jews do not need to become Christians to attain salvation. Kenneth A. Myers, writing in *Christianity Today,* an evangelical publication, calls the two-covenant theology essentially heretical because "there is no other name [than Jesus] by which we are saved." The founder and executive director of Jews for Jesus explicitly calls the two-covenant theology heresy, stating that "from the time of the early church, the Jews have been the most Gospel resistant people" and concluding that "persecutions of the Jews, instead of becoming a reason to cease telling Jews the gospel of God's love in Christ, should have become an impetus to do that."

* * *

The primary reason for religious toleration, such as through the Council of Churches, is to end religious wars. It isn't working, and logically, because of the central concept of all religions, it can never work. All religions differ, and no matter how slight the difference, to fundamentalists the dogma of all others is heresy, blasphemy, and cause for damnation.

Not only Catholics but also Protestants continue to disfellowship or excommunicate members. Jehovah's Witnesses, with some eight million members, disfellowship them at the rate of about seventy thousand per year; two-thirds of these never return. The most publicized cases are parents who are cast out because they allowed their child to undergo a blood transfusion. When one father's daughter died, the family members who remained Jehovah's Witnesses were forbidden by their church to attend the funeral. Members remaining in the church are ordered to avoid contact with disfellowshipped members. The result is referred to as "spiritual death." According to one former member, "many face the breakup of their family and are turned off to God and organized religion. Many end up suicidal." Grounds for disfellowship include smoking, excessive drinking, adultery, accepting a blood transfusion, joining the military, voting, and disagreeing with the teachings of their leaders. The Jehovah's Witnesses disfellowship anyone found to be associating with another disfellowshipped person or even speaking to him. They reject the idea of an afterlife, heaven, or hell, except for 144,000 lucky survivors mentioned in Revelations. They've been persecuted worldwide for their refusal to join the military and were sent to death camps in Nazi Germany. Jehovah's Witnesses look forward to Armageddon, which they predicted in 1914, 1925, and 1975. They have been accused of covering up multiple sex abuse cases because they interpret the Bible to require two witnesses for any transgression.

In *An Historian's Approach to Religion,* Toynbee

analyzes the inherent difficulties of religious tolerance:

> "The fruit of Pharisaism is intolerance; the fruit of intolerance is violence; and the wages of sin is death. The Mahometans [Islam], according to the principles of their faith, are under an obligation to use violence for the purpose of bringing other religions to ruin; yet, in spite of that, they have been tolerating other religions for some centuries past. The Christians have not been given orders to do anything but preach and instruct; yet, in spite of this, from time immemorial they have been exterminating by fire and sword all those who are not of their religion . . . if the infidels [non-Christians] were to agree to submit to a competitive examination in

which the marks were to be awarded for intelligence, for learning, and for the military virtues [sic], we ought to take them at their word; for, on these terms, they would inevitably be beaten at the present day. On all these three points they are far inferior to us Christians. We enjoy the fine advantage of being far better versed than they are in the art of killing, bombarding, and exterminating the human race."

Religious conflicts continue unabated in the Middle East, particularly between Sunni and Shia Muslims as exemplified by the wars between Iraq and Iran and the wars in Syria, Lebanon, and Yemen, with Christians and Jews involved in each of these wars. Sunnis constitute 87–90 percent of Islam, the most conservative including ISIS, theoretically defeated, and Wahhabism in Saudi Arabia, the two being almost indistinguishable.

A true brotherhood of the species can succeed only when organized religion disappears, but its disappearance should neither be expected nor its prohibition advocated, because outlawing religion would be as effective as outlawing any other superstition.

Religion and Sexuality

It's difficult to update the word of God. Our religions codified societal attitudes toward women when their holy books were written, between 1,300 and 5,000 years ago, when women were chattels. Consider the impact of God's saying to young girls through the holiest of holy books that they are fit only for bearing children and keeping their mouths closed (unless ordered to the contrary), always subservient to the male. These teachings are reinforced by parents, Sunday school teachers, and the minister; they govern behavior related to sex, including marriage, divorce, contraception, and sexual relations. Thus, it's easy to see why women have taken centuries to gain a modicum of equality with men. Yet female equality is far from realized, even in the United States.

According to Kinsey, the most important impact on a woman's sexuality is her degree of religiosity, no matter the religion. A third of unmarried devout Catholic women experience orgasm, while almost three-fourths of nondevout unmarried Catholic women do so; the same ratio holds true after marriage. Devoutness appears to promote masturbation and homosexual activity among women as safe alternatives to conventional sex outside marriage.

Research by Masters and Johnson found that religious orthodoxy is the prime indicator of sexual inadequacy. For

144

many religious women, sexual dysfunction becomes a way of life. Many develop "pelvic anesthesia" after marriage, or vaginismus, a psychosomatic condition wherein the pelvic muscles become so constricted that coitus is impossible. Most (if not all) such women are the products of a strict religious upbringing.

Most aspects of sex, especially outside marriage, are condemned as sinful by religious authorities. Most conservative or fundamentalist religions are against sex education, masturbation, coitus outside of marriage, coitus within marriage unless for procreation, prostitution, birth control, homosexuality, and divorce. Many religions instead favor celibacy, frigidity, and impotence, unless the object is offspring.

The Catholic church historically recognized a single allowable position for intercourse, male dominant. Other positions were deemed too animalistic, failing to confirm male dominance, or suspected of retarding conception. Pleasurable intercourse was sinful, as stated by Benedicti, echoing Saint Jerome, in his *La Somme des Pechez* (1601): "The husband who, transported by immoderate love, has intercourse with his wife so ardently in order to satisfy his passion that even had she not been his wife, he would have wished to have commerce with her, is committing a sin." (Rather like Jimmy Carter, who admitted lusting in his heart and was still elected president. Compare Donald Trump.)

The church regarded contraception as a major sin, equivalent to murder, requiring penances ranging in length from three to twelve years. Oral and anal intercourse were considered contraception methods. Coitus interruptus required two to ten years' penance. Penances required fasting (bread and water only) and abstinence from sex and other pleasures. Abortion was considered slightly less sinful if accomplished within forty days of conception, after which the fetus acquired a human soul. Because abortion was highly dangerous it was considered to carry its own penalty; still, Saint Jerome called women procuring abortions "threefold murderesses: as suicides, as adulteresses to their holy bridegroom Christ, and as murderesses of their still unborn child." You'd think birth control would be preferable.

A 2016 study by the Department of Psychology and Philosophy at Texas Women's University found that "Religious commitment is associated with decreased sexual activity, poor sexual satisfaction, and sexual guilt, particularly among women." Kinsey concluded that 75 percent of all divorces include sexual problems.

The parishioners of those religions prohibiting divorce were less likely to divorce than the more liberal Protestant and Jewish religions, probably from fear of excommunication. Should a person be forced to remain in a personally abusive or emotionally destructive relationship because a religion threatens excommunication as the alternative? Religiously oriented people suffer greater trauma and guilt from divorce.

Sexual repression affects mothering roles, particularly in pregnancy, childbirth, and nursing. Amenorrhea, the psychological suppression of menstruation, avoids adult sexuality and conception, lessening sexual anxiety. Many physical disorders associated with pregnancy are related to sexual anxiety, such as excessive vomiting and weight gain.

The earliest formative periods of a child's life may be molded by the mother's aversion to sex, much of which is religiously related. Many women who don't nurse are too embarrassed or too modest. Aversion to breast-feeding is related to a dislike of sex and nudity. Nakedness is equated with shame (Exodus 32:25; Revelations 3:18, 16:15).

However, a 2018 *Psychology Today* article found that the majority of "swingers," or wife-swappers, were religious; and a majority were Republicans. So much for stereotypes. Many participate based on a desire to overcome religiously engendered inhibitions; many women reported a decrease in guilt and an increase in self-esteem, a connection confirmed by other studies of sexual fulfillment and self-esteem.

* * *

Muslims, like Christians, blame the ills of the world on women because of Eve's role in causing the ouster of

Adam from the Garden of Eden. Women are punished by Islam in eighteen ways, paralleling those traditional in Christianity, ranging from segregation during menstruation to delaying remarriage upon widowhood. The Ottoman Turks, upon conquering Constantinople in 1453, embraced the harem, the secrets of which were kept until the death of the last sultan in 1909. Outside the harem, women were required to be veiled; inside the harem, they were virtual prisoners. Westerners always thought the harem was filled with hundreds of semi-naked women, heavy perfume, cool fountains, soft music, and all possible physical pleasures. Instead the harem consisted of between three and twelve hundred women learning housekeeping and coffee-making. One woman would become the mother of the next sultan and, if sufficiently strong, the ruler of the empire. During the early medieval period, thirty-five of the thirty-eight caliphs were sons of foreign slave girls. The ascendance to power guaranteed cutthroat competition among harem women with sons, as each mother vied to gain the favor of her son by the sultan. The alternative to the son's succession to the throne was death; a fifteenth-century law of Muhammed II required fratricide so that all brothers were killed when the next sultan was chosen.

Women's place in Islam is to serve at the pleasure of men. Not until 2017 did Saudi Arabia allow women to vote in governmental elections, and the first driver's licenses were issued to Saudi women in 2018. (When, prior to the lifting of the ban on female driving, forty-nine defiant Saudi women drove cars in Riyadh, they were threatened with serious punishment, and six were suspended from their teaching positions at King Saud University.)

The status of women in Judaism is that of "other," unclean or sinful. The role of Jewish women in the synagogue and Jewish society is subordinate; their place is in the home. Judaism is dominated by men and admits of no unflawed heroic women; as hard as God tried, he couldn't create an obedient woman. Women in the Bible are greedy, slothful, envious, frivolous, coquettish, gossipy, jealous, light-fingered gadabouts. (See Isaiah 3:16 and Genesis 18:10, 30:1, 31:19, 34:1.) The near-heroic women featured in these texts are belittled. Jewish women are raised to be wives and mothers, not adult human beings.

The Jewish male's Morning Prayer is "Blessed art thou, O Lord our God, King of the Universe who has not made me a woman." The corresponding female prayer ends in "who has made me according to Thy will." The prayer for a newborn male is for "Torah, marriage and good works"; the female prayer is for "reverence, marriage and good works." Women cannot lead Orthodox services or read from the Torah. In many synagogues men and women sit separately. Women are body, and men are spirit. Some of this inequality arose from the difference in marriageable

149

ages: twelve and a half for women and late teens or twenties for men. In Talmudic times women referred to their husbands as "Rabbi," a term used by a slave or student to refer to the master; men referred to their wives as "my daughter."

Historians trace a direct relationship between the Judaic patriarchal family structure, the concept of women as chattels (Exodus 22:16), and the double standard giving men sexual freedom with none for women. The characterization of women in the Bible is black and white, good woman and bad woman, temptress and virgin; the distinction is sexual activity.

A preoccupation with menstruation permeates Judaism. An orthodox Jewish woman may have no contact with her husband during menstruation, and he is forbidden on pain of sin to look on her face or form and must daily thank God he was not born a woman. These aren't relics of a barbaric past but the facts of Orthodox Jewish life today.

* * *

The Greeks invented lusty gods. Aphrodite was born from the foam on a wave of semen and bore Hermaphrodite, with both male and female sex organs, and Priapus, who was always erect. Heracles bedded fifty virgins in one night, including his nephew Jolaus and "Hylas, he of curling locks." Pederasty was preferred with sixteen-year-olds but banned with boys under age twelve. Higher education in

Greece from 600 to 400 B.C.E. featured an older male mentoring young lads, the same as in Buddhist Japan in the tenth century C.E. Plato's ideal of love was based on pederasty. Women in Greece were second-class citizens or slaves, permitted neither political nor legal rights. The Greek female gods were all flawed, similar to the women in the Old Testament. However, the Greeks invented dildos for female pleasure and accepted lesbians.

When the male was discovered to be necessary for procreation, the dominant goddesses were replaced by male gods. Woman evolved from a tiller of the soil (man was the hunter) and earth mother to become a chattel of the male. Women were first considered chattels of their fathers, then their husbands, and finally their sons. The oldest profession was not prostitution but priesthood. Priests gradually became the procurers of prostitutes operating in the temples.

In Sumerian times no stigma was attached to prostitution. Prostitutes provided substantial income for the temple and were required to remain unveiled. The Egyptians finally banned prostitutes from their temples; meanwhile, Solomon had seven hundred marriages and wives, making Liz Taylor look like a piker. Augustine said prostitution was shameful and immodest but necessary: "Yet remove prostitutes from human affairs, and you will pollute all things with lust; set them among honest matrons, and you will dishonor all things with disgrace and turpitude."

Thomas Aquinas said, "Take away prostitutes from the world, and you will fill it with sodomy." Thus, temple prostitution continued in Europe, limited to servicing Christians.

The status of European women changed drastically between 1100 and 1550, when females were elevated from a sex despised by men and themselves to that of respect and veneration as a mother figure. The Crusades brought fresh ideas to Europe and decimated the supply of men. With the men off crusading, women controlled and ran the great estates, surprising themselves and the remaining men by doing very well. The Byzantine idealization of the Virgin Mary was adopted, replacing the concept of all women as the seductress Eve. Courtly love began, and women became ladies. This new culture was derived from the Arab Muslims and resulted in romance poetry and troubadours singing of romance and beauty. Chivalry was born.

The hunt for evil women began at the same time—the hunt for witches. In the fifteenth and sixteenth centuries thousands of women were executed. In the small Swiss canton of Vaud, 3,371 women were killed as witches between 1591 and 1680. Wiesensteig, Germany, a small town, burned sixty-three women in the single year of 1562; in two years Obermarchtal burned 7 percent of its population as witches.

Pope John XXII emphasized the hunting of witches,

followed by papal decrees decrying witches in 1374, 1409, 1418, 1437, 1445, and 1451. Saint Augustine and Saint Thomas Aquinas believed miracles were caused by high magic and that witches wielded low magic. Heresy and sorcery were linked in the 1300s. Women were accused of making a pact with the devil, which allowed them to fly up chimneys after having been greased with the fat of slaughtered infants, whose blood they drank. They flew on broomsticks, spindles, or goats to meetings of witches at midnight on Thursdays, worshiping the devil in the form of a large black bearded man, or a goat, or a toad. They ritually kissed the goat under its tail or the mouth of the toad, had sex orgies, and ate human organs. The details varied by locale. Witch hunts centered in Germany, Switzerland, and France, later spreading to the fledgling United States.

A witch's existence was proved by torture, growing out of the Inquisitions, thus fulfilling the Biblical prediction that witches are to be killed. Certain women were automatically considered witches; wise women, midwives, and folk doctors; poor women, spinsters, and widows not subject to male control. Whole families of women were burned——mother, daughter, cousin, aunt, and grandmother. About 80 percent were women; the male witches were cripples or the handicapped, criminals, and relatives of female witches. The new Protestants were worse than the Catholics in hunting down and exterminating witches, particularly in England. Luther, Calvin, and Zwingli believed in witches. The craze died with the Inquisitions, but the Inquisitions didn't end until the 1800s.

The Bible is the basis for painting women as witches. See Deuteronomy 18:11–12 and Exodus 22:18, the latter of which says, "Thou shalt not suffer a witch to live." Pope Innocent VIII in the fifteenth century endorsed *The Witches Hammer,* coauthored by Inquisitor Springer, which provided:

> "The very word *femina* (woman) means one wanting in faith; for *fe* means "faith" and *minus* "less." Since she was formed of a crooked rib, her entire spiritual nature has been distorted and more inclined toward sin than virtue. . . . It is thus clear why women especially are addicted to the practice of sorcery. The crime of witches exceeds all others. They are worse than the devil."

John Wesley said, "Giving up belief in witchcraft is in effect giving up belief in the Bible."

The church opposed anesthesia for women during childbirth because Genesis 3:16 says, "I will greatly multiply thy pain and thy conception; in pain thou shalt bring forth children." Women were burned alive for seeking anesthesia. As stated by Elizabeth Cady Stanton, "The Bible and the church have been the greatest stumbling blocks in the way of women's emancipation. . . . The whole tone of church teaching in regard to women is, to the last degree, contemptuous and degrading." This should not be surprising, since 99 percent of our religions are founded on morality codified before the Dark Ages.

* * *

Let your women keep their silence in the churches; for it is not permitted unto them to speak; but they are commanded to be under obedience, as also saith the Law. And if they will learn anything, let them ask their husbands at home: for it is a shame for women to speak in the church.

I Corinthians 14:34–35

The ordination of women is a controversial subject in most religions. When the Church of England voted in 1992 to allow female priests, a thousand priests responded by threatening resignation. (The measure passed in early 1994, and by 2010 female priests outnumbered men.)

The ancient Christian prohibition against women teachers was reiterated by the Vatican in 1977. The Vatican stated it didn't "consider herself [sic] authorized to admit women to priestly ordination," refusing to consider the Virgin Mary as the equivalent of an Apostle, stating that only priests have a "natural resemblance" to Jesus Christ and that for a female priest "it would be difficult to be seen in the minister the image of Christ." Saint Paul said that because Eve had beguiled Adam to sin, her wages were silence forever.

Although the Catholic church prohibits female priests, the monthly magazine *U.S. Catholic* found in 2018 that 76 percent of its readers would welcome female priests; a third felt perpetuating an all-male priesthood was sinful; and 69 percent felt Jesus would have ordained women. A majority of the respondents were women.

The Origins of Celibacy

By the Roman period, religion was a branch of government, where as a practical matter it remains today. For example, all churches, no matter their origins, are exempt from government taxation in all countries on earth.

The historic threads of Christianity were Babylonian realism, Hebrew absolutism, Greek Platonism, and Roman materialism, resulting in Christian forgiveness, an absolute single god, platonic dualism, and money-seeking materialism. Constantine's declaration of Christianity as the official religion in 316 C.E. was a political move to unite the decaying empire, and it worked, though not to the benefit of Rome. Less than one hundred years later, in 410, Rome was sacked by Alaric the Great, imposing the Dark Ages until the Renaissance. The church became the empire and confirmed itself as the successor to imperialistic Rome when it began the Crusades.

During the Dark Ages only the church, with threats of hellfire, had the ability to enforce law and order. Only church leaders could read or write, which resulted in censorship, then called revealed truth. Sin was based not on New Testament concepts but on the writings of Jerome and Augustine, who reacted to the excesses of the Roman Empire. Jerome urged celibacy for all, which was considered ascetic compared to Roman sexual perfidy and materialism. He wrote in the fourth century, "I should like every man to take a wife who cannot manage to sleep alone because he gets frightened at night." People responded by embracing celibacy. Origen of Alexandria castrated himself in response to Matthew 19:12, which instructs men to "make themselves eunuchs for the kingdom of heaven's sake."

Saint Paul said that celibacy was superior to marriage and denounced prostitution because in sex "the two shall become one flesh" (1 Corinthians 6:15–16). Paul concluded it was better to marry than to burn with desire but advised married couples, in order to better enjoy prayer, to abstain from sex for one season a year. The church held that men from the waist down and all of women were the product of Satan. Christian folk legends called sex "an experiment of the serpent" and marriage "a foul and polluted way of life." (Both Jerome and Augustine were former sinners who had lusted after women. Augustine had prayed, "Give me chastity—but not yet.") The church fathers called intercourse fundamentally disgusting: "filthy and degrading" (Arrobas), "unseemly" (Methodius), "unclean" (Jerome), "shameful" (Tertullian), and "a defilement" (Ambrose). The church regarded sex as acceptable only before the fall; pre-fall sex in the Garden of Eden was considered cold and mechanical for the dual purposes of procreating and showing appreciation for the act of creation. The sin of eating the apple from the tree of knowledge caused selfish impulses in humankind, which, as a result, seeks filthy sexual pleasure with uncontrolled lust. Upon expulsion from the Garden we became aware of our nakedness and covered it to avoid willful activities by our genitals, requiring fig leaves to cover the pudenda, which derived from the Latin *pudere,* "to be ashamed." Every act of coitus was sinful, and resulting children were born into sin. Accordingly, Jesus was required to be born free of sin, without there being an act of sex, *ergo* the virgin birth by the Virgin Mary.

In 386 C.E. Pope Siricius decreed no intercourse between priests and their wives, to no avail. Abstinence orders by the church were lost in church corruption; but by the eleventh century Gregory VII was able to prohibit clerical marriage. The German priests declared they'd rather give up their lives than their wives, and they did. Still, the unenforceable church rules on celibacy were ignored by most. The church blamed families on Satan, calling children a bitter pleasure and denigrating wives as weak, slow, unstable, deceitful, and untrustworthy. A virtuous husband rejected his wife's advances, and vice versa. The church decreed that sex was unnecessary to marriage, though it allowed for procreation if practiced infrequently. The devout were required to abstain on Thursdays in memory of Jesus' arrest, on Fridays in memory of Jesus' death, on Saturdays in memory of the Virgin Mary, on Sundays in memory of the resurrection, and on Mondays in commemoration of the dead. Tuesdays and Wednesdays were largely wiped out with the ban on intercourse during feasts, festivals, the forty days before Easter, Pentecost, and Christmas, and the seven, five, or three days before Communion, ad celibacious. The admonition in the Old Testament to "be fruitful and multiply" was interpreted to help hurry along the Messiah. Since he had already arrived there was no more need for sex. Also, with the Christian era, women found themselves with the added burden that divorce was prohibited.

Celibacy and the Priesthood

Celibacy has been required of Catholic priests since the Second Lateran Council of 1139, the same council that began the Roman Inquisition. The celibacy of priests has been reaffirmed by the church as a "countercultural force," to prove there's more to life than the pursuit of pleasure. In October 1991, Pope John Paul II instructed priests to "follow the path that Jesus Christ opened, embracing voluntarily and joyfully the gift of priestly celibacy." A twenty-five-year study based on interviews with fifteen hundred people, however, revealed that about 40 percent of U.S. priests ignore their vows of celibacy. According to the study, done by R. W. Richard Sipes, a former priest, 20 percent pursue heterosexual behavior, 10 to 13 percent are homosexually active, and 6 percent are involved with minors. One-third of those interviewed were priests undergoing psychotherapy, one-third were priests sharing their stories in workshops or informally, and one-third were lovers of priests. The study also found that only half of priests generally support the idea of celibacy, and only 2 percent fully achieve required abstinence from masturbation. Secular psychology deems sex to be normal, healthy, and necessary to well-being. The International Synod of Bishops stated in response that celibacy shows there is "more to life than the pursuit of personal satisfaction." Up to 23 percent of priests are homosexually oriented, though only half of these are active sexually.

Celibacy and loneliness cause many priests to abandon their parishes. The retirement of Catholic priests, according to a statement in 2018 by the Association of Catholic Priests, has led to a decline in the number of priests from 58,632 in 1965 to "about 37,000. . . . The Catholic population has increased from 48.5 million to 74.2 million . . . while attendance at Mass has declined from 55 percent of all Catholics in 1965 to 23 percent in 2017. Out of 17,156 parishes in the U.S., more than 3,500 have no resident pastor. Laypeople and deacons administer 347 parishes."

In 2018 the Pew Research Center found that 76 percent of Catholics in the United States wanted the church to allow birth control and 62 percent wished the church would allow priests to marry (up from 58 percent in 1983 and 49 percent in 1971).

The celibacy required of Catholic priests has shoehorned the Catholic church into condoning pedophilia by refusing to investigate allegations of sex abuse by priests or to condemn priests convicted of child molestation. In

2018 a Pennsylvania grand jury found that 301 priests in a single diocese had molested over one thousand children during the last seventy years, all covered up by the Catholic church. Thousands of priests have molested tens of thousands of children in Europe: Belgium has over three hundred cases, with thirteen children committing suicide as a result. In September 2018 Archbishop Carlo Maria Viganò accused the pope of covering up the abuse and asked for his resignation. The pope urged "silence and prayer," while several American bishops described the complaining archbishop as "a man of integrity" without mentioning the pope.

Christians are more concerned with sexual issues other than priestly pedophilia, such as prayer and sex education in public school, birth control, nude sculpture, divorces, and television programs. A Vatican theologian, Cardinal Eduard Gagnon, told U.S. Catholic bishops that it's crucial for Americans to follow church teaching on sexuality instead of allowing Planned Parenthood, feminism, divorce courts, and spicy TV programs to dictate American tastes in sex. The meeting participants criticized divorce courts as "not fully in conformity with church law," criticized feminism as having "a deleterious effect on the family," and said theologians are recognizing "the social and moral disaster a contraceptive mentality can lead to." Planned Parenthood was accused of "encouraging promiscuity" and undermining Catholic teaching, although an estimated 80 percent of American Catholics use birth control. Priestly pedophilia wasn't mentioned.

In a 2017 interview with the German newspaper *Die Zeit,* Pope Francis was asked about the shortage of priests. He referred to the idea of *viri probati,* in which married or unmarried laymen recognized as potential leaders are ordained as priests, saying, "We have to reflect about whether the *viri probati* are a possibility. Then we also have to determine which tasks they could have, for example in far distant parishes. . . . In the church, it is always important to recognize the right moment, to recognize when the Holy Spirit demands something. That is why I say that we will continue to reflect about the *viri probati.*" The pope also discussed the possibility of female deacons, saying that theologians should study the example of Scripture. "What did this mean at that time [of the Bible]? What does it mean today?" He added: "Don't be afraid! That makes us free."

Religion and Homosexuality

A gay relationship is rarely used in religion as an example of perfect or divine love, though homosexuality is as physically natural as heterosexual relations. Instead, most religions picture gays as depraved, sinful, and shamed, as in the biblical term "sodomite," and seek to sever gay relationships, which is the same as ordering gays to separate or divorce. Paradoxically, gays have been the spiritual leaders and shamans of civilization since ancient times, until abhorred by the Catholic church in the twelfth century. They are welcomed in the West by a few denominations, such as Quakers and Unitarians. Wikipedia maintains a current list of religions that welcome gays, totaling a few percent of the world's thousands of religions. Other religions and society in general treat gays as outsiders, not belonging to church, family, society, or the workplace.

The American Psychiatric Association declassified homosexuality as a mental illness in 1973, and in 1975 the American Psychological Association resolved that "homosexuality per se implies no impairment in judgment, stability, reliability, or general social or vocational capabilities." Research by sociologist Frederick Whitam revealed that "homosexuality occurs at the same rates with the same kinds of behavior" in places as culturally diverse as the United States, Central America, and the Philippines; he concluded that the source is biological. The Kinsey studies found that people fall into seven general categories of sexual orientation, ranging from exclusive preference for the same sex to exclusive preference for the opposite sex, with many in between.

More recently, a June 2018 study released by the *Journal of Developmental and Behavioral Pediatrics* found there to be no difference between the psychological adjustment and prosocial behavior of gay parenting, whether by male or female parent teams, and heterosexual parents, based on "three groups of Italian parents: 70 gay fathers who had children through surrogacy, 125 lesbian mothers who had children through donor insemination, and 195 heterosexual couples who had children through spontaneous conception."

Most people biased against gays rely on religious orthodoxy, which holds homosexuality to be a sin. The pope actively condemns homosexual acts. Because the pope is infallible and in direct communication with God, his condemnation causes guilt in gays and hatred of gays. Homosexuals are held by many to be a proxy for evil and are faced with an open and intractable hatred associated with no other minority.

AIDS has given bigots an excuse to express their homophobia. The Catholic church has debated long and hard whether God is punishing AIDS sufferers but concluded that the best they could do was urge compassion for AIDS sufferers while rejecting the use of condoms or needle-exchange programs to control the spread of AIDS among intravenous drug users. The bishops concluded that chastity before marriage and fidelity within marriage are the only "morally correct and medically secure" means of preventing AIDS. Cardinal O'Connor stated, "The truth is not in condoms or clean needles. These are lies, lies perpetrated often for political reasons on the part of public health officials . . . by some health-care professionals who believe they have nothing else to offer persons with AIDS or [those] at risk . . . lies told by well-meaning counselors."

These condemnations are rooted in the Judeo-Christian heritage, driving gays from religion. Although two tenets of Western religion are unconditional goodness and love of God for all, this doesn't apply to gays. Instead, the Vatican has declared gays to be "objectively disordered" and "inclined toward evil."

Psychologists believe that the largest basis for homosexual bias is a combination of fear and self-righteousness by considering homosexuals a threat to basic morality. Male homosexuals were condemned by Pope Gregory III as harboring "a vice so abominable in the sight of God that the cities in which its practitioners dwelt were appointed for destruction by fire and brimstone," a creative interpretation of Genesis 19:4–11. Christianity was combating the favorable attitude toward homosexuality held by its predecessor, Mithraism, which had prevented the ban of homosexuality for hundreds of years after Christianity became the state religion.

The favored church punishment for homosexuality was castration and display of the offender with mutilated genitals. Saint Thomas Aquinas later "proved" that homosexuality was unnatural, thus lustful and heretical. His analysis was confirmed by the 1976 Vatican *Declaration on Certain Questions Concerning Sexual Ethics,* which is also followed by the United Presbyterian Church of the United States, Episcopalians, and Methodists. Thus, from the fourteenth century, homosexuals have been condemned in the West. Homosexuals were banned in France longer than witches; the last bonfire of a homosexual in France occurred in 1725. Homosexuality carried the death penalty in Great Britain until 1861 (seldom enforced), when the punishment was reduced to ten years to life in prison, and legalized in 1967 for consenting adults, except for those in the army, navy, or police.

Fundamentalist religions excommunicate gays. Antonio Feliz converted from Catholicism to Mormonism when his parents told him to, and thus grew up a Mormon, becoming a bishop to a Utah ward and writing speeches for then-president and prophet Spencer Kimball. Mormons, however, consider homosexuality a chosen lifestyle and upon discovering Feliz was homosexual, excommunicated him. A spokesman for the Mormon church commented, "Chastity before marriage and fidelity to your marriage partner during marriage—that's the Lord's standard and that's the Church's standard." Feliz points out that the Book of Mormon doesn't mention homosexuality, though it does teach tolerance and love, and that the founder of the Mormon church, Joseph Smith, "was sealing [marrying] men to men."

The Mormon church issued a statement in 1991 that all sexual contact outside of marriage, including "homosexual and lesbian behavior, is sinful. Those sins, though portrayed as acceptable and even normal by many in the world, are grievous in the sight of God." (Similar to Islam, Mormons believe in sex after death and that God has a goddess with whom he is sexually active.)

Gays and such behavior as turning away from a particular God are almost always blamed for any disaster, such as Jerry Falwell said after 9/11: "I really believe that the pagans and the abortionists, and the feminists, and the gays and the lesbians who are actively trying to make that an alternative lifestyle, the ACLU, People for the American Way, all of them who have tried to secularize America—I point the finger in their face and say, 'You helped this happen.'" The same scapegoats were cited for causing Hurricane Katrina, the 2011 Japanese tsunami, and many other natural disasters since Sodom and Gomorrah. In mid-1992 the Vatican formally declared its support for discrimination against homosexuals in public housing, health-care benefits, and employment as teachers, coaches, and military personnel. The Vatican said that "sexual orientation does not constitute a quality comparable to race, ethnic background, etc., in respect to discrimination," even though 78 percent of U.S. Catholics in 1992 favored equal job opportunities for homosexuals, up from 58 percent in

1978, according to a spring 1992 Gallup poll. By 2017 the Pew Research Center found that 67 percent of Catholics in the U.S. supported same-sex marriage.

The Christian repression of medicine has also colored Christian attitudes toward male homosexuals. The church insisted on trust in prayer and miracles as the only legitimate means to overcome disability and disease, because disease was caused by evil spirits as a punishment by God for sin. That conclusion continues with fundamentalist religious pronouncements on AIDS, transgender folks, and those who would use bathrooms allocated to a different gender from the one that was entered on their birth certificate at an age when it's difficult to discern sexual proclivities. The United States Catholic bishops rejected safe sex as a means to combat AIDS or to curb overpopulation.

The Centers for Disease Control found that most American high-school students have unprotected sex, though 95 percent know that unprotected sex risks AIDS and other venereal diseases. AIDS is the second leading killer of men and the fifth leading killer of women ages twenty-five to forty-four, and it is growing most rapidly among teenagers.

After four years of debate, the largest branch of Judaism, with 1,560 rabbis and 1.5 million members, voted in June 1990 to welcome sexually active gays and lesbians as rabbis. The Reform rabbis concluded that "for many people, sexual orientation is not a matter of choice . . . and therefore not subject to change. . . . Sexual orientation is irrelevant to the human worth of a person." Opposition to the move was based on Leviticus 18:22, which says, "Thou shalt not lie with mankind, as with womankind. It is abomination," and the scriptural admonition to be fruitful and multiply. Others countered that the scriptures cannot be taken literally; otherwise prostitutes must be stoned to death.

With the legalization of gay marriage by the U.S. Supreme Court in June 2015, attitudes toward the LGBT community softened. By 2018, the opposition to gays had dropped to 50 percent in the general population, with the overwhelming majority of younger and educated people supporting gay men and lesbians. A 2018 Gallup poll found two of three Americans approved of same-sex marriage, which was legal in twenty-eight countries, recognized in several others, and found to be a basic human right by the Inter-American Court of Human Rights. Even Catholics and other conservative religions were promoting LGBT tolerance—but not gay marriage. Conservative Judaism was in transition, with some acceptance of the LGBT community and same-sex marriage while, according to *The Advocate*, "most Orthodox rabbis oppose marriage equality and would not officiate at a same-sex wedding or affirm same-sex relationships," though some orthodox synagogues accept LGBT members.

Although same-sex marriages aren't generally sanctioned by most religions, individual churches within particular denominations can and do consecrate same-sex couples, including the United Methodists, the Unitarian Universalists, and the mainly homosexual Metropolitan Community Church.

In 2018 the Vatican said the LGBT community "must be accepted with respect, compassion, and sensitivity, and every sign of unjust discrimination in their regard should be avoided," but the only choices offered to gays by most religions today are to change their orientation, remain celibate, or engage in a spurious heterosexual marriage.

With the election of Donald Trump as president in 2016, the percentage tolerating gays began to drop by several points a year. In 2018 a Harris poll found that the Catholic tolerance of the LGBT community, which had risen for four consecutive years, had dropped by 2 percent.

The mainstream Protestant denominations that ordain openly gay ministers constitute a continuing entry in Wikipedia, numbering approximately twenty out of the world's thousands of religions. Most of these are state churches in Europe. The issue has created schisms in the U.S. Episcopal, Lutheran, and Presbyterian churches and, according to a 2017 article in *Salon,* could split the Methodist church as well.

* * *

Today, U.S. Catholic bishops denounce sexism as a sin but continue to defend the church's refusal to ordain women as priests. The bishops have praised the work of Christian feminists but warned against "radical feminist groups," which advocate "such aberrations as goddess worship, witchcraft, liberation from conformity to the sexual morality taught by the Church or the acceptance of abortion as a legitimate choice for women under pressure."

The independent news site *Crux*, which covers the Vatican and the Catholic church, cited two actions by Pope Francis in 2018 that suggest the Me-too movement was a turning point for the church: "a concession that any priest can forgive the sin of abortion, not simply a bishop or priest specially designated by the bishop, while the second is the elevation of the feast of St. Mary Magdalene to the same level as those of the male apostles." The article went on to say that the church admits some practices have "depersonalized and depreciated women," leaving them as "objects of suspicion, condemnation, condescension, or simply ignored."

Bishops support female deacons and altar servers but uphold the male priesthood and bans on artificial contraception. Notwithstanding the discrimination against women in religious seminaries, the only reason enrollments haven't dropped precipitously is the influx of women beginning in the 1970s. By 1985, a third of those seeking ordination in mainline Protestant seminaries were women. Religions that prohibit the ordination of women are experiencing a crisis in the decline of their clergy. The population of Catholics in the U.S. grew by 15 percent in the last twenty years, while the number of graduate-level seminarians fell by half. The shortage of priests has forced some Catholic churches to merge and others to close. U.S. Catholics are importing priests from the Philippines, Haiti, Korea, and India. Some Catholic leaders believe this influx stalls long-term solutions to the shortage problem, such as opening the priesthood to women and married men. Over 3,500 U.S. Catholic parishes have no priest, and the number of new priests has halved since 1965, from 1,000 a year to fewer than 500.

Protestants and Jews are experiencing a similar crisis, though at a lesser level because of women enrollees in their seminaries. More liberal Protestant sects, such as Episcopalians, generally support the ordination of women ministers. Although more women are being ordained by more denominations, in proportion to men they receive fewer job offers and lower-level jobs upon ordination. The real problem isn't getting the first job, which is usually available as a college chaplain or assistant, but by the third job change women fall significantly behind male clergy in the size of church and salary. More churches are open to women pastors, but many balk at accepting a second woman pastor for fear of becoming known as a woman's church. The nature of religion is such that if it changes at all, it changes glacially. The problem is how to change infallible doctrine without revealing it as fallible.

* * *

Some Protestant churches are changing their attitudes toward sex. In 2018 the Presbyterian church issued a revolutionary document on sexuality suggesting it "adopt a new ethic, one that measures sexual relations on the basis of mutuality, honesty, consent and fidelity"—all elements of what the church calls "justice-love." On this ethical basis, the church observed, even marriages may "offer the exciting potential of confronting and transforming patriarchal patterns of dominant-subordinate relating." But just as marriage is not necessarily related to "justice-love," neither, in the report, is intercourse related to the procreation of children. Indeed, pregnancy is barely mentioned except as something to be avoided through contraception or abortion. Thus, for a denomination that has already declined by half a million members over the last two decades, the report sounds a call for widening the circle of faithful—not with children but with nonreproductive gays, lesbians, and heterosexual singles who practice "safe sex." The church sold 27,000 copies at five dollars each, making it a Presbyterian best seller.

Only when it comes to sex and sensuality do most

churches preach absolute literalism of Bible scriptures. Churches are torn between considering their flock as innocent babes to be kept in their pristine state forever or as the innately sinful who will eventually scandalize the church with sexual excesses: oppressive rules guarantee rebellion. The familial relations of a primitive tribe of Hebrews thousands of years ago, predating the Dark Ages and now carved into the Bible, have little connection to much of anything, much less modern standards of love and sex.

The Separation of Church and State

Romans 8:1–2 states there is no power except God; such power is ordained by God, and resisters to this power are damned. The U.S. Constitution, on the other hand, states that all political power is inherent in the people, who retain the inalienable right to alter the government as they deem fit. The impetus for exclusion of God from the U.S. Constitution came from George Washington, Ben Franklin, James Madison, Ethan Allen, Thomas Jefferson, and the Adamses. George Washington wrote into a treaty with Tripoli, "The government of the United States of America is not, in any sense, founded upon the Christian religion."

Yet religion is an integral part of our politics. Many legal holidays in most countries are religious holidays, including the two most important holidays in this country, Christmas and Thanksgiving. Even secular holidays, such as the Fourth of July, Memorial Day, and Labor Day, feature religious representatives on reviewing stands and celebrations opened by blessings and prayer.

The reason Utah has no lottery and will never have a lottery is that its legislators are Mormons, and the religion forbids gambling, alcohol, smoking, and caffeine. Accordingly, the Utah Constitution says: "The Legislature shall not authorize any game of chance, lottery or gift enterprise under any pretense or for any purpose." Yet, every Utah poll since 1985 has favored a lottery.

In 1989 the 11th Circuit Court of Appeals in Atlanta declared prayers before school-sponsored events to be unconstitutional; the ruling was uniformly ignored in Georgia, Florida, and Alabama, the states within the 11th Circuit. When the U.S. Supreme Court let the decision stand by refusing to review it, prayer continued before high-school football games in this Bible Belt region. The mayor of Childsburg, Alabama, led those attending the season opener in prayer: "We thank you, Lord, that we do live in a free land, a free land where we can pray. Bless us now, keep our players safe." Police confiscated a banner stating that church and state don't mix, saying it was prohibited by city ordinance.

A 2014 poll by the Pew Research Center for its Religion and Public Life Project found that "nearly half of Americans believe religion should play a bigger role in U.S. politics." Forty-nine percent of respondents wanted to see houses of worship express their views on political and social issues, and 41 percent believed political leaders do "too little" when it comes to praying and expressing their religious faith. The poll also found an increase in the number of people who say they believe churches should be allowed to endorse candidates for office. Thirty-two percent felt that way, even though such partisan activity is a violation of the federal tax code's prohibition against campaign intervention by houses of worship.

Most U.S. presidents invoke God regularly. "God bless you and God bless the United States" has become a presidential mantra since President Reagan closed his last address to the American people with those words.

The tradition of the National Prayer Breakfast, a 90-minute round of prayer and testimonials hosted by the president at the Washington Hilton, began in the Eisenhower years. President Reagan declared 1983 the Year of the Bible, giving fundamentalists leverage to promote prayer in public schools. When the U.S. Senate declared 1990 the International Year of Bible Reading, President Bush and eighteen state governors endorsed the campaign to have one billion people read the Bible, nonstop, from Genesis to Revelation.

* * *

Arnold Toynbee, in *An Historian's Approach to Religion,* described the impact of the failure to separate church and state:

> "The effect of this
> capture of higher religions for
> alien mundane purposes has
> been doubly disastrous. On

the one hand the captured higher religions have been diverted from their true mission of preaching a new gospel in which God is revealed as being Love. . . . Whole-heartedness can rise to sainthood when it is directed to the religious purpose that is its true end, but it is apt to descend to demonic savagery when it is prostituted to the service of mundane causes."

President Bush proclaimed a National Day of Prayer before the Persian Gulf War, asking millions of Americans to pray for divine aid in what he called a "just war." Bush had an approval rating of over 80 percent during his "just war," which resulted (though difficult to tell exactly) in excess of 80,000 civilian deaths. Meanwhile, Saddam Hussein declared God to be on Iraq's side in a "holy war" against the Western invaders.

In 2018 President Trump led a god-and-country speech at the National Prayer Breakfast. "We can all be heroes to everybody, and they can be heroes to us," Trump said. "As long as we open our hearts to God's grace, America will be free, the land of the free, the home of the brave and the light to all nations." He concluded, "Our rights are not given to us by men, our rights are given to us from our creator. No matter what, no earthly force can take those rights away."

Mark Twain's *The War Prayer*, written during the Philippine–American War, portrays Christian prayer in wartime. It begins:

> "It was a time of great and exalting excitement. The country was up in arms, the war was on, in every breast burned the holy fire of patriotism; the drums were beating, the bands playing, the toy pistols popping, the bunched firecrackers hissing and spluttering; on every hand and far down the receding and fading spread of roofs and balconies a fluttering wilderness of flags flashed in the sun; daily the young volunteers marched down the wide avenue gay and fine in

their new uniforms, the proud fathers and mothers and sisters and sweethearts cheering them with voices choked with happy emotion as they swung by; nightly the packed mass meetings listened, panting, to patriot oratory which stirred the deepest deeps of their hearts . ."

And this is how *The War Prayer* ends:

"Lord our Father, our young patriots, idols of our hearts, go forth into battle— be Thou near them! With them—in spirit—we also go forth from the sweet peace of our beloved firesides to smite the foe. O Lord our God, help us tear their soldiers to bloody shreds with our shells; help us to cover their smiling fields with the pale forms of their patriot dead; help us to drown

the thunder of the guns with
the shrieks of their wounded,
writhing in pain; help us to lay
waste their humble homes
with a hurricane of fire; help
us to wring the hearts of their
unoffending widows with
unavailing grief; help us to
turn them out roofless with
their little children to wander
unfriended in the wastes of
their desolated land in rags
and hunger and thirst, sports
of the sun flames in summer
and the icy winds of winter,
broken in spirit, worn with
travail, imploring thee for the
refuge of the grave and denied
it—

"For our sakes who
adore Thee, Lord, blast their
hopes, blight their lives,
protract their bitter
pilgrimage, make heavy their
steps, water their way with
their tears, stain the white

182

snow with the blood of their wounded feet!

"We ask it, in the spirit of love, of Him Who is the Source of Love, and Who is the ever-faithful refuge and friend of all that are sore beset and seek His aid with humble and contrite hearts. Amen."

This is a religion that has as a principal commandment "Thou shalt not kill." Where is it written "unless a politician tells you to kill someone you have never met and though that person has done nothing to you"?

In his book *The Deaths of Others: The Fate of Civilians in America's Wars,* research scientist John Tirman analyzed our attitude toward civilian casualties and concluded that Americans don't care about the lives of foreign civilians. U.S. military forces slaughtered over six million innocent civilians—the equivalent of the entire population of Los Angeles and Houston—in Korea, Vietnam/Laos/Cambodia, Iraq, and Afghanistan, and that's a conservative estimate.

Consider what each of those wars accomplished:

Korea: The conflict that led to the division of North and South Korea resulted in almost 34,000 American casualties; civilian and other military casualties totaled 2.8 million. The repercussions of that long-ago war continue today with the threat of mutual nuclear annihilation.

Vietnam: Fifty-eight thousand Americans and almost 600,000 Vietnamese died. We dropped two million tons of bombs during 600,000 bombing missions over Laos (more than all the bombs in WWII), killing over 50,000 civilians and creating minefields of unexploded ordinance that is, even today, responsible for hundreds of deaths per year. What did this accomplish? What would be the American reaction if another country slaughtered half a million U.S. civilians, as we did in Vietnam? Compare 9/11, when the deaths of fewer than three thousand American civilians resulted in outpourings of patriotism, yet we don't give a thought to the literally millions of innocent civilians we've killed. However, the Vietnamese hold no grudges, at least the ones I've talked to in Vietnam. They consider the American war a blip in time, compared to the centuries of conflict with China and the decades of battling the French.

Iraq: Household surveys put the civilian death toll in excess of 500,000, and notwithstanding the theoretical end of that war the total rises every single day. Do we care?

Afghanistan: Seventeen years of war have led to more than 100,000 civilian deaths, and the count rises daily. Our longest war ignores historical reality in a region of the world that has been a graveyard for foreign powers, from the Great

184

Game waged between the British and the Russians in the nineteenth century to our inept arming of the Taliban in 1979 to counter the Russian invasion. When the Taliban took over Afghanistan in 1996, its prohibitions, detailed in the penal code, included, "pork, pig, pig oil, anything made from human hair, satellite dishes, cinematography, and equipment that produces the joy of music, pool tables, chess, masks, alcohol, tapes, computers, VCRs, television, anything that propagates sex and is full of music, wine, lobster, nail polish, firecrackers, statues, sewing catalogs, pictures, Christmas cards." By 2018 the Russians were bankrolling the Taliban against the Americans. Those who ignore history repeat it, over and over and over.

Our frontier myth that righteous violence is necessary to subdue local savages, often called terrorists, governs much of our foreign relations, along with a Second Amendment gun-slinging attitude at home. The U.S. military code for the operation to capture Osama Bin Laden was "Geronimo," perhaps a mere historical coincidence.

These basic facts are not taught in our schools. Instead we continually thank our troops for their service in theoretically protecting the U.S. from invasion by every country from Vietnam to Afghanistan, Grenada and Panama, while our public schools teach "creation science," prescribe "voluntary prayer," and fail to mention the atrocities of the dominant U.S. religions that tortured and executed millions

185

of people over centuries.

* * *

Until the United States Supreme Court decided the *Texas Monthly* case in 1989, religious property in forty-five states was exempt from taxation by local and federal governments. In addition to giving churches a broad exemption from property taxes, California and Idaho exempt meals from sales tax when served by a religious organization; Georgia, South Dakota, and Washington exempt tax on sacramental wine; Virginia and Missouri charge no tax on church-owned automobiles; and Mississippi exempts from its amusement tax those programs "consisting entirely of gospel singing and not generally mixed with hillbilly or popular singing." The cost to government from revenues lost by these exemptions is substantial and must be made up by other taxpayers, which means we're all required by law to subsidize religion, including those godless religions other than our own.

In its *Texas Monthly* plurality opinion, the Supreme Court held that a state may not constitutionally exempt church books and publications from sales tax. Three justices opposed any special privileges for religion; three tolerated a nodding acquaintance, without explaining how big a nod is allowable; and the other three varied according to the circumstances. The *Texas Monthly* case has signaled a gradual severing of the two-hundred-year special symbiotic relationship between government and organized religions.

Does God Exist?

> To many Americans . . . a drought . . . is the will of God,
> and they flock to the churches to pray for rain under the
> impression that the plans God has made are so trivial and
> unimportant that He will change them if asked to do so.
> —Isaac Asimov, *Extraterrestrial Civilization*

A person asserting the existence of a fact always has
the burden of proving the asserted fact. If a plaintiff sues on
a contract, it's up to the plaintiff to prove the existence of the
contract and not up to the defendant to prove its
nonexistence. One reason the law operates in this fashion is
that a negative, or the nonexistence of a fact, cannot be
proved. Therefore, the burden of proof lies where it
belongs—on the person asserting the fact or the existence of
a particular god. Unfortunately for theists, no argument for
the existence of God has met any measure of proof. The four
primary arguments for the existence of God are internally
illogical.

Notwithstanding acknowledged deficiencies,
organized religions cling to the arguments for the existence
of God analyzed below, and no others. *The Catholic Word
Book* notes that "the First Vatican Council declared that the
existence of God and some of his attributes can be known
with certainty by human reason, even without divine

revelation."

The first argument is the "first cause" principle, based on the seemingly logical argument that everything is caused by something, and therefore the universe must have been caused by God. The illogic of the argument is evident upon its statement. Even assuming that everything does have a cause (unprovable), there is no necessary connection with the universe being created by a particular god or any god at all, since that assumes that gods exist. The universe could have been created by little fairies, a sociopath (seemingly likely), aliens, microbes, or a trillion other suppositions. The Christian version of God is an omnipotent, omnipresent, perfectly good, all-knowing, and disembodied spirit. There is no logical necessity that the creator of the universe be omnipotent, omnipresent, good (or even nice), all-knowing, or a disembodied spirit. In fact, if our unending wars are included in God's plan, he appears to be a sadistic jerk.

The first-cause argument contains the insupportable assumption that the creator of the universe came from outside the universe. One difficulty with the argument is that if we concede everything must have a first cause, then God must have a cause, and there appears to be no answer to the question of who created God. No matter what, something was created out of nothing, unless the universe has always existed.

The second argument for the existence of God is the

"design" argument. Because nature is ordered and rational, with strict operating rules, the argument is that someone must have designed it and that someone must be God. The chief illustration used to support this argument is that of a watch with its exact machining and internal intricacies, which leads to the inescapable conclusion that it had a maker. The maker is so wonderful that he must also have a maker and that maker must be God. The argument stops short without revealing its implicit conclusion that man's wonderful maker, God, could have no maker.

The design argument assumes that a complex inanimate object proves the existence of a God, instead of the existence of an animate object, such as a cat or a tree, or even man. What is necessary to prove or disprove the existence of God? Does the fact that all human and other animals have legs exactly long enough to reach the ground prove the existence of a God? A chair may be used to barricade a door, or a tree branch as a walking stick, or a dead cat as a boomerang. Does a particular use prove the existence of a particular creator or any creator at all? The design argument provides as much support against the existence of God as for it, which is to say, no support one way or the other.

A more logical (scientifically supportable) argument is that evolution is the sole creator of the design, so that, given enough time, life itself evolves and continually refines itself within the design of nature. Does this exclude the possibility that a God programmed evolution into nature to do God's work, creating life and the human species? Of course not, but it remains both remote and speculative without discernible logical support. It would seem absurd to conclude that humans are the culmination of God's handiwork, for if that were true, then we have a defective God who has created a far from perfect handiwork. He created Hitler, Stalin, and the Indians who slaughtered Custer, all of whom may be considered good or bad, depending on our individual viewpoints.

Kant logically solved the complaint that God could not have created himself with the hypothesis that God is outside the universe and thus not subject to the rules of causality. Kant's hypothesis begs the question, though, because there is no reason not to as easily accept the hypothesis that the universe just happened. There is no support for either theory, and the short answer is that we simply don't know. Man, however, has evolved the faculty of logical deduction and the talent for judging statistical probability, and when we come right down to it, after examining all the evidence, the existence of a God appears beyond remote.

The third argument is that God must exist simply because we have the concept of God. Just because we have a concept, however, does not mean the thing exists—witness unicorns (maybe they did exist and maybe God is dead), werewolves (ditto), Elvis rising from the dead (or any other entity rising from the dead), and multiple other examples.

The fourth argument for the existence of God is that there must be a basic lawgiver because humans are cognizant of basic moral principles. Absolute moral law requires an absolutely moral mind, or God. The logical difficulties with this argument are numerous. Probably no two people in the world can agree on ten moral precepts. The simplest and clearest moral concept, that we shouldn't kill other human beings, is riddled with exceptions recognized by most religions: war, execution of criminals, self-defense, mercy killing, and the withdrawal of life support from the hopelessly ill (though many religions dispute even this). Thou shalt not kill, except in lots of circumstances. The conclusion is that there may be no such thing as absolute morality, or at least none on which everyone can absolutely agree.

The laws of nature cannot imply a lawgiver because natural laws are descriptive, not prescriptive, such as would be made by a lawgiver or legislature. Prescriptive laws are those of ethics and religion—do this and do not do that— quite different in kind from the laws of nature. Simply because God might be a possible cause of the laws of nature doesn't mean that God probably or certainly is. The existence of natural laws also doesn't mean that they are the only possible laws. There could easily be infinite variations so that gravity would cause objects to fall a foot per second faster or slower, ad infinitum. All variations, from the point of chance, are equal and are as probable as there being no laws at all, i.e., chaos. If God exists, he would do so whether the universe is orderly or chaotic; the ordered state of the universe adds no support to an argument for the existence of God.

Notwithstanding the uniform rejection of these arguments by logicians, *The Catholic Word Book* definition of God uses these arguments as the basis for proving the existence of God:

> "The existence of God is an article of faith, clearly communicated in divine Revelation. Even without this Revelation, however, the Church teaches, in a declaration by the First Vatican Council, that men can acquire certain knowledge of the existence of God and some of his attributes. This can be done on the basis of principles of reason and reflection on human experience.

"Non-revealed arguments or demonstrations for the existence of God have been developed from the principle of causality; the contingency of man and the universe; the existence of design, change and movement in the universe; human awareness of moral responsibility; widespread human testimony to the existence of God."

Contemporary Catholic theologians characterize God as unknowable, even in heaven. In his book *Geist in Welt* ("Spirit in the World"), Karl Rahner expresses the idea that the only way to understand God is through pure belief, "loving self-surrender" or "loving obedience," but God even then and in heaven remains undecipherable:

"Even when the human spirit has been elevated to the supernatural order [i.e. goes to heaven], God remains its mysterious Horizon, whose unobjective presence is

necessary for every act of
knowledge, but who is never
understood himself. God
remains the Free Creator who
can be known only through
the dynamism of the human
spirit's loving self-surrender
to him. Because God can be
known only through an act of
loving obedience, the
Christian Mystery is
essentially religious."

Science-fiction writer George Zebrowski, in an article
for *Omni* titled "Life in Gödel's Universe: Maps All the
Way," compared similar closed and ultimately unknowable
systems:

"Nothing can ever
count against it. A trivial
example: Little green men
live in all refrigerators, but
they disappear when the door
is opened. Another example is
a religious dogma of any kind,
held on faith. Both of these are
what [Karl] Popper calls

'reinforced dogmas,' because they have a built-in resistance to any kind of test; they contain as part of the idea an injunction against questioning them. . . . Dogmas are the enemies of Gödel's universe because they attempt to *end* all discussions and tests of truth; they are totalitarian viruses for the mind, preventing the creative growth that Gödel's proof implies is possible. . . . Completeness is a form of death; wildness is a form of fertility, growth."

No proof for the existence of God has ever been offered that would be admissible in any court of law. Only faith supports a belief in God. Religious faith and superstition are indistinguishable, two areas of human life that cannot be supported by rationality or fact. If God existed, shouldn't there be some shred of evidence somewhere of a force defined as all-pervasive and powerful? It's insufficient to argue that the existence of God explains everything for which we have no other explanation. It is far more honest to say, "I don't know," than to say, "God did it," particularly since no one "knows" whether God exists, or whether any of the gods of our thousands of religions exist.

The existence of miracles is based on identical logic, according to their definition in *The Catholic Word Book* as events that "cannot be explained by the ordinary operation of laws of nature and which, therefore, are attributed to the direct action of God." Ignorance of natural causes is not the equivalent of nonexistent natural causes. An explanation given without supporting proof is the same as any explanation, or no explanation, and is equally valid.

There are cogent arguments against the existence of God that arise directly from the Christian definition of God. A main one has to do with the existence of evil. If God is omnipotent, if he can do anything and win any battle or contest, then why does evil exist? Is God willing to prevent evil but unable to do so, and thus, not omnipotent? Or is God able to prevent evil but unwilling to do so, and therefore indistinguishable from evil? The Christian answer is that God is so far above us as not to be understandable in these terms, which is no answer at all. If we stray from the path of logic, there is no hope for our kind. In an illogical world good is equal to evil and nothing makes sense.

It appears impossible that a good God would permit

197

evil. For example, why would God will the death of an infant in a burning house? If such is God's will, then why should society punish the arsonist who set the fire and was merely doing God's will? Can we defend God by saying he is good, and therefore the evidence against him is misleading because in the long run the baby's death was all for the good? If a bystander could have saved the baby from the burning house without harm to himself but did not, would we call the bystander good? What kind of God is it that could have saved the baby from the burning house but refused?

The religious answer is that babies trapped in burning houses are necessary to create moral urgency in mankind. Should we then abolish firefighters so God won't have to personally set more fires when moral urgency falls below a certain level? Is the arsonist a hero in creating moral urgency? Moral urgency could be further maximized by abolishing the medical profession and hospitals, and we could become Christian Scientists. There would be no reason to promote peace, prevent famine, and wipe out disease; we could return to the Middle Ages, when religion ruled all. If there is an excuse for God to allow disasters and deaths of infants, what is it? Picture the infant in the burning house and God observing from afar as the flames lick the crib, and then the sheets. It's not too late for God to wave an incorporeal finger and save the baby. What reason could God have for sitting on his incorporeal behind as the flames explode and envelop the screaming child? Does it matter whether such a God exists?

A fundamentalist answer for the existence of evil is Satan. Unfortunately, no religion specifically describes the origins of this prince of darkness and Satan's inherent inconsistency with the tenets of the Christian religion. When God created everything, why did he create Satan? Was God too young at the time and didn't realize the havoc he was releasing on the world, or was God stupid? The devil is not mentioned in the Old Testament, though devils are mentioned numerous times; Satan is mentioned three times with no reference to his origins (masculinity of Satan is assumed). There are thirty mentions of the devil or devils in the New Testament, including Christ giving authority over devils to his disciples (Luke 9:1), making devils subject to Christ (Luke 10:17), and stating devils believe in God and tremble (James 2:19). If these passages are correct why does God or Christ tolerate such devilish evil? The New Testament says that Satan is to be transformed into an angel of light (2 Cor. 11:14) and that one thousand years after the Second Coming he is to be let out of prison (Rev. 20:7). Why does the devil receive only a one-thousand-year sentence while human sinners are relegated to hell for eternity?

If God is all-powerful, why doesn't he kick the devil's butt and be done with the scamp? Who created the devil, apparently as the equal of God? Surely God didn't create the

199

devil. If so, God must be somewhat less than infallible, since he picked Satan as one of his angels, arguably one of the monumental God-blunders of all time. If God had the devil in a pit, why did he let him out again? Inattentiveness? How did Satan "force" God to send his son to earth? The logical answer to any of these questions appears to destroy the credibility of the Christian religion. An illogical answer is neither creditable nor worthy of belief.

Another alternative answer to the God/evil question is that evil is only the absence of good and God is not responsible for the absence of good. If so, then what is God responsible for and what kind of God is that? Another answer is that evil brings man to spiritual health and maturity. It appears more logical to conclude that evil (and life) brings death and that the proponents of the argument should reread George Orwell's *1984,* particularly the parts on "doublespeak."

Another argument is that there's no accounting for good if there's no God. Would it be equally logical to conclude that there's no accounting for evil if there's no Satan? Does the existence of beauty, fidelity, or friendship mandate the existence of a particular supernatural being? What does one concept necessarily have to do with the other?

The probability that the Christian God exists (or the radically differing gods of our thousands of religions) is equal to the probability of the existence of the gods of ancient Rome, Greece, and Egypt, or the gods of Jonestown, Babylon, and the Clan of the Cave Bear. Logic can neither prove nor disprove the existence of the Christian God or any other "God."

What if, as logic may dictate, there is likely no God? If there is no God, we need not bow and scrape and crawl before the images of a nonexistent God; we need not follow the arbitrary rules of organized religion that make life on earth miserable and foment endless conflicts and wars and plunge the uneducated and third world into direst poverty by prohibiting birth control; we could discard our primitive superstitions.

Science, Religion, and Censorship

Why do all religions look for historic verification of their dogma and never find it? Consider the Shroud of Turin and the search for the Ark on Mount Ararat. There is no evidence that anything described in the Bible ever occurred. It would be remarkable if the Bible were accurate, because it is admittedly made up of oral traditions recorded decades after the occurrences purportedly described. The Old Testament appears to be a Hebrew folk myth, similar to the Christian folk myth of the New Testament.

The Bible excludes any mention of education. The root of all sin is Adam and Eve eating from the Tree of Knowledge. The Christian religion teaches that the truth is fully known, a principle that limits inquiry and fosters superstition. Anyone who disagreed with religiously ordained truth was historically considered a heretic. The "educational" issues most often raised by religions today are whether to allow prayer in public school, release-time for religious studies, sex education studies, and similar issues unrelated to education itself.

In 2017 more than 1.2 million children dropped out of U.S. high schools, one every twenty-six seconds or seven thousand a day. Eighty percent of New York high school graduates can't properly read or do math, and 40 percent of American high schoolers don't graduate with an aptitude for either college or work. Sixty percent of those graduating don't know enough to fill an average entry-level job. However, the percentage of students "graduating" from high school more than doubled, from about 40 percent in 1960 to almost 90 percent in 2017.

In his best-selling book *A Brief History of Time,* Stephen Hawking wrote that the pope personally instructed the world's leading physicists to stop talking about a big bang because the universe was created by God. Mr. Hawking ignored the pope and concluded that the universe likely had no creator, which means the spirit in the sky that religion calls God does not exist. Religion responded swiftly. At a "Heavenly News" gathering in Washington, D.C.'s National Cathedral, an astronomer noted the similarities between the big bang theory and Genesis 1:3, which says, "And God said, let there be light." At the same conference a theologian said the creation depicted in Genesis was never intended as a statement of scientific fact but was an act of worship demonstrating the exiled Jewish community's belief in order amid the chaos of exile. Christian leaders, as reported by the Associated Press, announced that the "Big Bang supports science and religion." However, a recent poll found that 42 percent of Americans thought God created humans in their present form in the last ten thousand years, 40 percent said we developed under God's plan over millions of years, and 9 percent said we developed without a god; 4 percent were undecided. The Associated Press concluded that facts change no one's mind.

* * *

All religions experience miracle cures and apparitions. According to the *Book of Lists 3* the Virgin Mary made 232 "confirmed" appearances in thirty-two countries (all to Roman Catholics) between 1928 and 1975. A miracle cured thousands of crippled and diseased peasants in Guatemala after they viewed an image of Christ that appeared on the side of a church. The faithful continued to believe even after a rainstorm revealed the image to be a Willie Nelson poster that had been covered by a recent whitewash of the church.

Muslims in England flocked to the house of a man who cut an eggplant open and found that the seeds spelled the name of Allah in Arabic. In the first month forty-five hundred pilgrims journeyed to the man's house to observe the seeds, and the town's mosque designated the eggplant a holy object.

A stray cat in Kuala Lumpur, Malaysia, appeared on its hind legs with its paws held forward and was regarded as a reincarnation of Buddha. The cat appeared regularly in a local prayer hall, perhaps to meditate.

The only consistent factor in all religious experience is that people only see symbols or beings from their own religious background. A Christian never sees Buddha in a vision and a Buddhist never sees Christ. Only Catholics see the Virgin Mary and only Muslims see the archangel Gabriel; only Taoists have religious revelations that all government is bad, though the rest of us may suspect it. This consistency leads to the conclusion that religious experience arises solely from the mind.

Since religious experiences likely arise solely from the mind, the question becomes how these experiences differ from seeing Casper the Friendly Ghost or pink elephants and whether such experiences more likely prove the existence of God than the existence of Casper or pink elephants. Is it relevant that the Bible repeatedly recognizes the existence of unicorns (Num. 23:22; Job 39:9, 10; Psalms. 29:6, 92:10), though biblical scholars now argue that the term was mistranslated for animals similar to large oxen? Does the existence of a headache prove the existence of Satan based on the religious explanation from the Middle Ages that a headache is caused by devils banging around inside the head? From a scientific point of view there is no difference between a man who eats too little and sees heaven and a man who drinks too much and sees snakes. Both result from abnormal physiological conditions.

* * *

Throughout history, where the Bible has ruled, the populace has been uneducated. In 1570, for instance, Philip

II forbade Spanish citizens to study outside of Spain, fearing Protestant influence; Spanish universities became no more than facades. All writings were censored. Shakespeare was scissored apart; adverse references to the church and its heroes were deleted. As late as 1800 there were few elementary schools in Spain. In 1896, only 30 percent of Spanish adults could read, and as late as 1927 a woman was sentenced to two and a half years in prison for saying, "The Virgin Mary had other children after the birth of Jesus." She had impiously relied upon Luke 2:7 and Galatians 1:19. In 1910 the church still prohibited education for women, on the grounds that education would harm them. Only by legally separating church and state has any form of government contained the excesses of religion.

Comparing religion to science, religion attempts to control without understanding, while science advances solely through understanding. A theologian gains "knowledge" through divine revelation, which constitutes absolute truth and, because everything is known, justifies a closed mind, creating thousands of absolute truths by our thousands of different yet infallible religions. *The Catholic Word Book* defines theology as "knowledge of God and religion, deriving from and based on the data of divine Revelation, organized and systematized according to some kind of scientific method." Theology, though, constitutes the opposite of a scientific method; a true scientist is always required to be open-minded and accept only truths that are proven.

Knowledge is defined as being based on evidence that establishes fact, not on belief without evidence. If religion had not controlled human society for the last five thousand years the human race would be advanced far beyond its present state of knowledge and science. Because the Bible teaches that the end is near, religion has never thought it appropriate to find out about the natural world. As stated by Caliph Omar when offered the remnants of the great Greek library at Alexandria, "If the books agree with the Quran, the Word of God, they are useless and need not be preserved; if they disagree with it, they are pernicious. Let them be destroyed." Fortunately, other Muslim leaders preserved Greek literature.

The movable-type printing press was invented in the 1500s, and for centuries thereafter the church required permits to print books. The Index Expurgatorius banned all books not acceptable to the church. Such censorship, of course, has been practiced by all religions.

Luther called Aristotle "a devil . . . a wicked sycophant, a prince of darkness . . . a beast, a most horrid imposter on mankind . . . this twice execrable Aristotle," because of Aristotle's scientific method.

When the church suppressed the scientific method, Islam exercised scientific leadership. Nobel Peace Prize winner Naguib Mahfouz, points out:

> In our victorious battle against Byzantium, [Islam] gave back its prisoners of war in return for a number of books of the ancient Greek heritage in philosophy, medicine, and mathematics. This is a testimony to the human spirit's demand for knowledge, even though the demander was a believer in God and what was demanded was the fruit of a pagan civilization.

The Christian churches still hold that truth is available only through divine revelation.

The steam engine was originally invented by Hero, a mathematician in 100 B.C.E., but all scientific progress was halted with the advent of Christianity and for centuries thereafter; the steam engine was finally reinvented in the 1750s by James Watt. Alexandrian mathematicians proved that all objects fall toward the center of the earth; this was not rediscovered until Newton in the seventeenth century. The study of physics was outlawed by Pope Alexander in

1163. Francis Bacon was excommunicated and imprisoned for discovering that many things attributed to demons were naturally caused. His discovery of the telescope and microscope was suppressed for centuries.

When Galileo contradicted the infallible Catholic church by claiming the earth was not the center of the universe but in fact revolved around the sun, he escaped burning at the stake by renouncing his theory with the following statement:

"I, Galileo, being in my 70th year, being a prisoner and on my knees, and before your Eminences, having before my eyes the Holy Gospel, which I touch with my hands, adjure, curse and detest the error and the heresy of the movement of the earth."

Galileo was tried twice during the Roman Inquisition, and his investigation was reopened by the church in 1980. His innocence was announced by Pope John Paul II at a meeting of the Pontifical Academy of Sciences on Halloween 1992.

By order of Pope Paul IV, the Catholic church began its index of banned books in 1538. The ban carried the death penalty for any bookseller violating it and was enforced in Spain until 1804. Many books had been banned before the Index was begun. By 1534 no book could be printed without church permission. Licenses were prohibited for printing translations of the Bible. All libraries were expurgated. In addition to Spain, the Index was enforced in Belgium, Bavaria, Portugal, Italy, France, and Germany. Italian science was the world leader before the adoption of the Index; it never recovered its preeminence. In 1619 Kepler was banned. Dante and Galileo were censored; many authors were hanged or burned. The Index also banned all works by Dumas, Hobbes, Hume, More, Proudhon, and Voltaire, as well as selected works by Descartes, Kant, Locke, Mill, Rousseau, Spinoza, Darwin, Defoe, Gibbon, Flaubert, Montaigne, Montesquieu, Diderot, Zola, and Stendhal.

The field of medicine has also suffered because of religious censorship. Medicine in the eyes of the Catholic church consisted of holy relics, which were (and are) used to generate revenue. The church resented any scientific advance that would depreciate its income from these bits of bone and hair. Relics are described in *The Catholic Word Book* as "The physical remains and effects of saints, which are considered worthy of veneration inasmuch as they are representative of persons in glory with God. First class relics are parts of the bodies of saints, and instruments of their penance and death; second class relics are objects which had some contact with their persons."

In the fourteenth century, Pope Pius V ordered doctors excommunicated if a priest was not associated with their medical treatments. Upon excommunication the practice of medicine was forbidden because the church controlled the state. Surgery was opposed because it interfered with the pureness of the body on resurrection day.

Jews and Muslims developed medicine during the Middle Ages. The plague was blamed on the Jews because their doctors taught sanitation and fewer Jews died. Accordingly, the Jews were executed for hexing Christians and causing the plague. Luther declared, "Satan produces all the maladies which inflict mankind." It was considered heretical to use quinine to treat malaria or to inoculate against smallpox. Muslims had discovered inoculations, but they were condemned by the Catholic church.

Religion hasn't changed. Children of Christian Scientists die because their parents believe in miracles and prayer and refuse to allow medical doctors to provide blood transfusions, even in life-and-death situations. Christian Scientists have been convicted of felony child abuse, involuntary manslaughter, and child endangerment in Arizona, California, Florida, and Massachusetts for withholding medical treatment from their children. An international spokesman for the sect claimed these criminal cases interfered with the First Amendment guarantee of religious liberty. Defense co-counsel in the Massachusetts case said, "We're literally talking about the extinction of a religion through this prosecution." The church ran a two-page ad in a Boston newspaper headlined, "Why Is Prayer Being Prosecuted in Boston?" An article in the *Journal of the American Medical Association* concluded that Christian Scientists die younger than the rest of the population, based on a study tracing the medical records of over thirty thousand members for fifty years. Several states have religious exemptions to criminal child abuse and neglect statutes, including at least six state laws that exempt parents from manslaughter. These exemptions were reexamined in Idaho after the state reported that five children had died unnecessarily in 2013 because their parents, for religious reasons, had refused medical treatment for them. A bill was introduced in the Idaho Legislature to repeal the manslaughter exemption, but it was defeated in the Idaho Senate in 2017. Thus, parents in Idaho and most states can deny medical treatment to their children and remain immune from any civil or criminal punishment though the child dies as a result.

* * *

In 2017, the Pew Research Center found that thirty-four states and D.C. offered a legal shield for parents who refuse medical treatment for children on religious grounds:

[Image: Religious Exemptions.jpg]

* States with laws that specifically mention Christian Science.

Note: Recognized category includes Pennsylvania, which specifies that beliefs must be consistent with those of a "bona fide religion." U.S. territories not shown.

Source: Pew Research Center analysis of data from the U.S. Department of Health and Human Services

According to CNN in 2018, "Evangelical Christian minister Gloria Copeland, who sat on the Trump campaign's evangelical advisory board, drew criticism for recent comments about avoiding flu vaccination: 'We don't have a flu season and don't receive it when somebody threatens you with 'everybody is getting the flu,' " Copeland said in a Facebook video. She claimed that Jesus was himself protection from the flu and suggested that people avoid the virus by repeating the phrase "I'll never have the flu."

"We've already had our shot," Copeland said. "He bore our sicknesses and carried our diseases. He redeemed us from the curse of flu, and we receive it, and we take it, and we are healed by his stripes, amen." Her comments came in the middle of one of the United States' worst flu seasons in recent years, one that killed dozens of children and resulted in the highest number of hospitalizations recorded by the Centers for Disease Control and Prevention.

* * *

Because we will never be in complete control of our environment, religion will always have its place. We all have a craving to understand, to trust our secular and religious leaders, and to believe they know, even better than we do, what is good for us. Religion is an explanation to adults such as adults give to children. Religion achieves security by promising infallibility and demanding belief.

As summarized by Ingersoll:

> Every church pretends
> to have found the exact truth.
> This is the end of progress.
> Why pursue that which you
> have? Why investigate when
> you know? Every creed is a
> rock in running water:
> humanity sweeps by it. Every
> creed cries to the universe,
> "Halt!" A creed is the ignorant

Past bullying the enlightened
Present.

Except for purposes of entertainment, only truth has value. There's no subject too sacred to investigate or understand. The inhibition of the search for truth in any area of life inhibits the progress of the species. We shouldn't reject fact on the orders of any person, whether king, president, or pope. No ideas are sacred but should all be subject to investigation and debate. The truth should not require us to cringe or bow in fear, to pray or to praise. Truth is. It can extinguish the flames of hell, the hypocrisy of fear, and the repetition of sacred shibboleths.

* * *

Our species is known for its superstitions. Gamblers resort to random numerology, such as betting odometer readings, license plate numbers, or the dates of birthdays and anniversaries. Stockbrokers are highly superstitious, which is logical considering the control they exert over the stock market, which is little more than socially acceptable gambling.

The National Science Foundation found in 2013 that 42 percent of Americans consider astrology to be scientific. A follow-up study found there is substantial confusion between astronomy and astrology. A 2003 poll found 51 percent of Americans believe ghosts exist, 68 percent believe Satan is real, and about half believe in the existence of hell.

Superstitions plagued our ancestors in the Middle Ages and made their lives miserable. There was no universal education; perhaps one in twenty thousand could read and write. There was no progress or invention, only religion and prayer. Priests were the shepherds of the people, bulwarks against knowledge, thought, and doubt. Human toil was used to support the useless pious and to build magnificent churches while their members lived in slums. For hundreds of years Christianity concentrated on wresting the empty sepulcher of Christ from the Muslims, killing millions, while the Christian God lost battle after battle.

Our products of value have come from science and the unreligious who abolished slavery (supported by many religious), clothed the poor, fed the hungry, lengthened our lives, secured our homes, and provided us with the richness of art, music, books, and travel. No advance in the betterment of our species has been driven by religion or superstition.

Superstition is not only a bad joke but a common human weakness because it treats "make believe" the same as reality, which is a children's game. Where religion dominates a people or nation they are governed by the unseen and unknowable, remaining children and never becoming adults. Human dignity is replaced by ritual and astrology, sacrifice and voodoo. Progress ceases and liberty ends. Superstition artificially sets one human above another—popes, priests, and preachers are holier than the rest of us. Superstition imprisons the virtuous, tortures thinkers, chains the body, and often seeks to stifle freedom of speech. A difference in opinion about a superstition counts as heresy and blasphemy. Superstition counts human love as degrading; it elevates monks above fathers, nuns above mothers, and faith above fact. Superstition creates an elitist heaven; a hell of eternal revenge; a world of unending religious conflicts and hatreds; an enemy of rationality, medicine, and science.

The connection between organized religion and superstition is illustrated by the study of any primitive people. The American anthropologist Alma Graham and her writer husband, Philip Graham, studied the Beng ethnic group in Ivory Coast for fourteen months. The villagers dressed similarly to you and me, lived in adobe houses, and entertained themselves with late-night storytelling instead of watching television. When Philip Graham found himself with writer's block, he did what any Beng villager would have done; he consulted a noted female diviner in a distant village. The diviner placed his previous writings on an animal skin, then held a brass pan with several black pebbles and water made milky by a white powder designed to draw spirits. She watched the pebbles and announced that the writer should sacrifice a white hen on the next sacred day, and then a goat. They then toasted with palm wine.

Graham followed the diviner's directions. An animist priest poured the chicken blood over the sticky roots of a sacred tree and then the blood of a goat. Graham started writing again, about the ceremony.

The Grahams' 1993 study (reprinted in *Braided Worlds,* published by the University of Chicago Press in 2012) showed that the world of spirits was used to explain every occurrence in the village, whether disease, insanity, or misfortune:

> "We were told of the spirits who lived in the tall iroko tree dominating the nearby coffee fields and who sometimes could be heard singing at night, a whistling wind. A hundred yards farther away in the rain forest was another spirit village, the home of a polygamous spirit man who flew at night from one invisible village to another, visiting each of his two wives, and whose path

was through our courtyard. The sound of the wind on those nights was the sound of his flight. Indeed, we discovered that the wind itself was the very movement and sound of all spirits, and in the forest encircling the village each swaying tree and shaking branch was their transfigured presence. Soon Alma and I grew attuned to the order of invisible things, as Kouassi [a friend in the village] carefully recounted to us the cosmology that was carried inside every person we passed on a village path or bargained with in the market; another universe in familiar bodies, and the multiplication, in a crowd, of strange, shared secrets. The spirits lived within the Beng and therefore around them as well, for those anterior presences also filled up their outer world."

The Beng experience is parallel to the voodoo experience of Haitian zombies, related by James Michener in his book *Caribbean*. Four certifiable zombies were under protection of the Haitian government, all zombified in the same manner. The zombie in *Caribbean,* Lalique Hebert, was seventeen years old when a jealous sister paid a voodoo *bucor* to "kill" her. The medical doctor rescuing zombies for the Haitian government described the zombie maker:

> "Like a bishop in the Catholic Church, who can claim a straight-line inheritance from Jesus Christ, he's a straight-line descendant of some notable native doctor in Africa. But he has to be extremely skilled in making nice distinctions. Too much of his magic powder, the target dies. Too little, the target does not pass into perfect suspension, comes awake too soon, suffocates in his grave."

The voodoo *bucor* has the knowledge of secret and

powerful poisons and drugs that can induce the suspension of life functions. The clinical death of the target is accurately certified by a medical doctor. The target is buried in a sixteen-inch--deep grave, dug up the second day, and resuscitated by the *bucor,* who keeps the resurrectee in a suspended state (by depriving the target of salt) and later sells the target as a slave in another region. Lalique Hebert had been a zombie slave for eleven years when she was discovered and slowly weaned away from her voodoo religious and drug-induced conversion. Her fellow villagers shunned her, reducing her to sleeping on the streets. The investigator asked the villagers where Lalique had been sleeping:

> "Maybe sleep here. Maybe against that wall. . . . Not good have zombie in village. She come for revenge, maybe. Someone here in bad trouble, maybe. . . . She try to stay, people drive her out. . . . Zombies go many places. They not need eat . . . sleep . . . think. Missy, they not like you and me."

The spirits around us have been harnessed by our

religions that worship gods indistinguishable from the Beng and voodoo spirits, residing within us and constituting the soul. How does any religion differ from the superstitions of primitive people? Both speculate about the unknowable with abiding fear. How is one distinguishable from the other? How can anyone intelligently decide the truth among Beng spirits, Catholicism, Judaism, Buddhism, voodoo, Taoism, or any of the thousands of religions, sects, and cults of the spirit, except to admit a preference for the traditional religion of our immediate ancestors? Our sole advancement in fifty thousand years has been our consolidation of various spirits into one spirit called God. Even this refinement, however, is illusory, because Western Christians still believe in billions of spirits—Father, Son, and Holy Ghost make three (or one) plus angels, saints (for some), devils, and souls numbering in the umpteen billions. Hindus revere 330 million gods, enough to provide every person in the United States with his or her personal god.

Why do we believe undocumented things with no supporting evidence? By 2019, it was difficult to believe that we care about facts. Do we? Perhaps we don't want to know, hoping what we don't know won't hurt us. An example of this can be seen in books by Robert Fulghum, such as *All I Really Need to Know I Learned in Kindergarten,* and *It Was on Fire When I Lay Down on It,* the latter of which contains the following epigraph:

"I believe that imagination is stronger than knowledge—that myth is more potent than history. I believe that dreams are more powerful than facts-—that hope always triumphs over experience—that laughter is the only cure for grief. And I believe that love is stronger than death."

Fulghum is undoubtedly correct. We're more comfortable with sustaining our beliefs instead of trying to reconcile them with contrary facts, which might start our belief systems crumbling from within. Then we would have to think for ourselves, and there is nothing more strenuous and disconcerting. For these reasons neither superstition nor religion will likely become less popular in the foreseeable future.

Many believe the universe operates on the principles of science as embodied in the forces of nature without the intervention of an invisible god or other unverifiable superstition. If there's no God, Christian or otherwise, that doesn't mean life is meaningless. Life is full of meaning, and so is death. Without death there'd be no evolution, no progress, and no change. Is the life of any animal meaningless because it dies? When faithful Fido dies has his life been without meaning? Is the significance of giving gifts diminished by the discovery that Santa Claus doesn't exist, or is gift-giving enhanced? What is required for meaning in life? Would there be more meaning if there were life after death, or would that simply be a longer life? Is there less meaning to a short and quality life than to a long and unhappy life? If in fact this is the only life we have, does its length matter, since our memories vanish when we die?

Without death we'd be forever suspended without the mechanism of natural selection and evolution to claw us upward. Our species would be frozen in space and time. Life and death force evolution to create a higher order. The meaning of life may be to create this higher order, to bring improvement to the species, and to the quality and quantity of life. We can perhaps evolve to a higher intelligence with better abilities to cope with one another, individually and within 193 nations and thousands of religions. Our increased ability to communicate across cultures and store information may speed our development geometrically. Or, of course, it may not because of conflicts, wars, and human greed.

There are many positive aspects to rejecting superstition. Everyone in the universe becomes equal. There are no lost souls or heretics to kill or convert. The only guideposts are sensory perception, logic, and science.

Whether God or gods exist becomes meaningless. Morality would be determined by conditions in this world without worrying about thousands of different ideas of an afterworld. There would be no personal immortality, no eternal hobnobbing with the gods, no guilt based on religious shibboleths, and no threat of divine anger. Human potential would be the touchstone of life. There would be no more delusion.

A Radical Theory of Morality

Moral indignation is jealousy with a halo.
—H. G. Wells

A primary reason for the severe reaction against a critical examination of religion is the assumption that without religion there would be no morality or ethics. This assumption is not only contrary to the evidence but historically absurd. More atrocities have been committed in the name of religion than in the name of Lucifer or any secular leader. Without organized religion the human condition would likely improve, together with morality and ethics.

If we threw out our organized religions, what would happen to the substance of the Ten Commandments? Nothing. Every civilized (and not so civilized) country in the world has codified the only ethical Commandments (four of the last five), the substance of which predated these Commandments by centuries: "You shall not commit murder. You shall not commit adultery. You shall not steal. You shall not give false evidence against your neighbor."

Where in the world is it, or has it ever been legal to murder, commit adultery, steal, or give false evidence, whether the local government is Christian, Jewish, Muslim, Taoist, Buddhist, Hindu, or Rastafarian? Yet Crusaders and

226

inquisitors in the Middle Ages, along with fundamentalists of all ages, instruct us to murder the infidel.

The lower animals act more ethically toward the members of their own species than we do. Horses don't organize armies to slaughter other horses, nor do any of the lower species. Is this because these species are insufficiently intelligent? Birds feed blind birds, and biologists find that the fittest for evolution are not necessarily the strongest but those that combine for mutual support. Creatures highly organized to cooperate include ants, bees, termites, beavers, muskrats, apes, parrots, and most lower animals. We seem to lack the ability to distinguish between citizens under the thumb of repressive governments and governments that our government considers the enemy. We similarly have difficulty in distinguishing between a particular religion and its adherents. We tend to stereotype others who differ by national origin (an accident of birth) or religion (mostly an accident of birth).

Social opinion is the greatest molder of conduct, for good and for bad. Humans have always been social, living in groups. A high level of cooperation was historically required for our survival, necessitating the development of ethics long before the codification of organized religions.

Many older societies have long traditions of hospitality—Bedouins, for example, as well as Arabs, Turks, and Afghans. There are minor differences in our moral codes, but most of our kind are highly ethical, except in our general attitude toward outsiders or noncitizens, those who are not our political allies. Most older societies were democracies, with the entire community or tribe participating in decision-making. Most of us are scrupulously honest, particularly those who've had little contact with Western man. It is mostly civilized people who steal from and defraud others. Most tribes have a limited idea of owning property, except for a few personal possessions, so there is little concept of stealing. The Carib Indians have a saying that if something is missing, "there has been a Christian here." Truthfulness is practiced more often in these "backward" societies than in our own.

The Golden Rule was in existence for hundreds of years before the Bible was thought of. It is found in the Mahabharata ("Treat others as thou wouldst thyself be treated") and in the teachings of Confucius ("Do to every man as thou wouldst have him do to thee; and do not to another what thou wouldst not have him do to thee. This perceptively dost thou need"). Aristotle said the same thing. Socrates was sentenced to death for corrupting the minds of the youth of Athens because he thought ethics was independent of religion. Ethics was the core of human society before Christianity and other religions were even thought of.

Although Muslim countries are far harsher on property

crimes than Western countries, the ethical four of the Judeo–Christian–Islam Ten Commandments are the core of the criminal law in all countries, including pariahs such as North Korea, Syria, and Iran.

The only Commandments that have made no inroads into the criminal law of any country are the six Commandments unrelated to ethics. The first commandment, prohibiting the tolerance of other gods, has caused the deaths of millions, fending off the heretics who believe in other gods, the foundation of Christian ethics:

> "You shall have no other god to set against me. You shall not make a carved image for yourself nor the likeness of anything in the heavens above, or on the earth below, or in the waters under the earth. You shall not bow down to them or worship them; for I, the LORD your God, am a jealous god. I punish the children for the sins of their fathers to the third and fourth generations of those that hate me. But I keep

faith with thousands, with those who love me and keep my commandments. You shall not make wrong use of the name of the LORD your God; the LORD will not leave unpunished the man who misuses his name. Remember to keep the Sabbath day holy. . . . Honor your father and your mother. . . . You shall not covet your neighbor's house."

The last two Commandments implicate thought "crimes," the failure to venerate father and mother or the coveting of the neighbor's wife.

* * *

Almost all religions, save a few recent ones, such as Scientology, founded their guiding principles before the Dark Ages, when our ethics were even more barbaric than they are now. The Bible is full of good and wise sayings and precepts mingled with foolish and horrific concepts, similar to the Quran and other holy books.

Slavery was upheld by all religions until less than two hundred years ago. Slavery is commanded by the Christian and Jewish Gods (assuming the two are dissimilar). Is slavery ethical, or is it moral only when it coincides with national policy, such as until recently in South Africa or in the United States 160 years ago? Segregation was the law in the southern United States fifty years ago and the hatred of others with a different shade of skin or flavor of religion continues worldwide and may never cease.

Of 37,000 Catholic priests in the United States in 2016, three hundred were black, which is slightly over half of 1 percent. The church blames the deficit on the lack of black seminarians and declining seminary enrollment by all races. Before Vatican II in 1965, however, blacks were barred from the priesthood and full participation in the church. Blacks couldn't receive communion until after whites had received it. The record of the Protestant churches is no better. The logical conclusion is that Christianity is racist, either de facto or intentionally, reflecting society as a whole. Based on my experience as a travel writer living in 170 of the 193 countries in the United Nations, every country in the world, without exception, discriminates against and looks down on its minorities.

War has been a mainstay of most religions since time began, and it continues to be so in the Middle East, from Syria to Yemen and Israel, in India and Pakistan, and all over Asia and Africa. The God of the Old Testament makes clear the just desserts for the other side in war:

"Every one that is found shall be thrust through, and every one that is joined unto them shall fall by the sword. Their children shall be dashed to pieces before their eyes; their houses shall be spoiled and their wives ravished. . . . Their bows also shall dash the young men to pieces; and they shall have no pity on the fruit of the womb; their eye shall not spare children."

Isa. 13:15–18

Slay utterly old and young, both maids and little children, and women.

Ezek. 9:6

Happy shall he be, that taketh and dasheth thy little ones against the stones.

Ps. 137:9

The books of the Old Testament are not books of morality and ethics but books of serial criminal activity.

They teach revenge, eternal pain and damnation, human sacrifice, and poverty as a condition to enter paradise, which no one has ever reported experiencing. Lest we think the Old Testament is repudiated by more enlightened Christians, we need only consider the numerous atrocities committed in the name of Christ throughout the last two thousand years and the prayer services on both sides before every war.

Traditional Morality Versus the Right Stuff

If religious beliefs are inaccurate guides to ethics and morality, what is the proper guide? Philosophers and the rest of us have been grappling with this problem forever. Empirically, morality varies between countries based on the maturity of the dominant religion. Americans and Europeans have dissimilar views about the morality of walking around naked at the beach   and yet both are primarily Christian. As a practical matter much of morality is relative. The core objection against relative morality is that it's not morality at all, but only a social or individual viewpoint. This argument concludes that truth cannot be based on viewpoint and neither can morality, otherwise, any individual view of morality would be correct, and, if my view differs from yours, either you are incorrect, or vice versa. However, religious doctrines are also relative because none of the world's thousands of religions agree on much of anything, and on nothing completely.

An overview of historical theories provides a foundation and an introduction to the inherent problems of knowing what action is ethical in all circumstances.

One early philosophical moral theory is hedonism, which teaches that pleasure is the primary good. The validity of an action is judged by the level of pleasure produced or the happiness obtained. Probably the most widely practiced ethical system is egoistic hedonism, which is represented by the question, "What's in it for me?" This may be the world's most popular ethical system. The Epicureans elevated hedonism to an arguably higher level by emphasizing physical health and peace of mind as the two purest pleasures.

Hedonism has been criticized as not being a moral system at all because it doesn't answer the question of what one ought to do. It simply says, "Be happy." Perhaps that's enough of a goal, but it neither provides a guide to happiness nor does it tell us what actions are moral in particular situations. However, once basic necessities are satisfied it may be an accurate description of the most common goal of our kind.

Another major defect of pure hedonism is that it doesn't prevent a person from bloodying your nose if that makes him happy. When combined with altruism, however, hedonism may be an acceptable moral system; i.e., the proper goal should be the happiness of others instead of merely one's own happiness. This combination is most likely unachievable and impractical because one can never (or seldom) know what will achieve happiness for others, when most (or certainly many) people don't know (particularly in a time frame greater than five minutes down the road) what will make them happy, and many of us are too busy to care. This system is summed up by the admonition to love our neighbor as ourselves and has had little historical success. Most of us seem to limit the idea of "neighbor" to the chap living right next door, and we aren't too sure about him.

A similar moral system that appears more practical, though it has at least one glaring defect, is utilitarianism, also called social hedonism: Seek the greatest good for the greatest number. Democracy is a related political system and suffers from the same defect—the minority is subject to trampling. Jeremy Bentham and John Stuart Mill debated the details of utilitarianism. Bentham emphasized the quantity of happiness for the most people and counted the individual as having only one vote in that calculus, which would consider the intensity of the pleasure, its duration, certainty, propinquity, future availability, purity, and number of people affected. Such a calculus is obviously unworkable as a practical guide for daily living. Mill argued that quality was more important than quantity and intellectual pleasure was superior to physical pleasure, which may exclude the majority of the population. Mill was an extremely bright guy, but he made the fatal assumption that everyone should be judged on the same intellectual basis as himself. Pleasures of the intellect may be illusory to half of the population, and Mill's theory excludes obvious pleasures of the flesh.

Another major theory of morality was proposed by Immanuel Kant, who posited that moral absolutes can be deduced by an appeal to pure reason and shouldn't be based on experience or ideas of happiness—a tenet of most religions. Acting in accord with one's duty is acting in accord with moral law, which is to say that one should only do those things that everyone should do: the Universal Imperative. Therefore, suicide would be unacceptable, as would hedonism. If everyone acted only for his or her own pleasure, there would be no progress and little morality. Kant's theory depends on the fallacious assumption that the full development of our talent is the only moral course. That may be a high ideal, but it is of little solace for civilians surrounded by armies girded for battle and those struggling for their next meal. A full 70 percent of the world's population—4.5 billion people—lives on ten dollars a day or less. The vast majority living in North America and Europe are filthy rich, comparatively.

My simplistic proposal for a practical system of morality is summed up in four words: Harm no one else. As long as we harm no one else, adults should be allowed to do exactly as we please, including risking harm to ourselves. If being an adult means anything it means being able to do exactly as we wish as long as we harm no other person. (I leave the treatment of animals, other than ourselves, to others.) Although it may appear simplistic and innocent, this is a radical theory of morality that flies in the face of every religion and system of government but avoids the defects of traditional theories of morality and provides a specific and workable guide for everyday living.

Simply harming no one else avoids the central defect of hedonism, which is if it makes you happy you should be able to bloody someone else's nose. It also avoids the impossibility of altruism, to make everyone happy when few of us know how to make ourselves happy, much less the rest of the world. Avoiding harm to others skirts the unworkability of utilitarianism, which relies on a complicated pleasure calculus that would stump a supercomputer. It also avoids the eternal question whether quantity or quality of pleasure is better and whether the calculus should be restricted to intellectual pleasure. It goes Kant's Universal Imperative one better by reducing it to one concrete commandment, which is based on experience and basic ideas of happiness. (It's a happy person who harms no one else.) It also avoids Kant's imperative that intellectual development is the only or highest good but fully allows and encourages such development. It pushes armies back from the brink of mutual destruction and negates the purpose of most government. It should be the law, the only law: Harm no one else (except in self-defense).

This can never be the law, however, as long as there are organized religions with contrary rules and arbitrary sins or when governments seek to regulate the aspects of their citizens' lives that harm no one else.

Harming no one else allows resources to be employed in the pursuit of individual happiness, similar to the unrealized principles espoused in the Declaration of Independence. Whether happiness for the particular individual is intellectual, physical, or of any other sort should be solely up to the individual, independent of religion or government.

The true test of any ethical system is equal treatment of all so that what is right for one is right for all. This is how we define justice and fairness. Immorality destroys well-being and happiness. The best guide to justice and fairness in lieu of organized religion or superstition appears to be intelligence and education. Only a good man is a happy man. No man is ultimately happy who is not good. Let whichever god you believe in out of our thousands of religions deal with the transgressors against your preferred god. He has the time and the means. Otherwise, interfere with no one who doesn't interfere with you and don't do unto others that which you would not like done to you, which is to say, harm them not.

However, a preliminary question is from whose viewpoint "harm" should be determined, that of the actor or from the viewpoint of the person being acted upon? The only workable solution is to prohibit only that which appears harmful from the perspective of the person threatened with harm. The fact that I think my action is harming no one is inconclusive if someone can show that they would be harmed by my action. Anything you wish to do should be allowed if no other person is harmed as a result, even though a person similarly situated would in the same circumstance feel harmed. Thus, adults should be allowed to engage in any activity (harming no one else in the process) if both wish to do so including risking harm to themselves as they deem appropriate.

How does harming no one else fare when applied to everyday situations and to the moral issues of our time? For instance, when can we justify a lie? When it harms no one else. We do it all the time; we lie to spare the feelings of another, which is to say we avoid harm to another. *The Catholic Word Book* dodges the issue in its definition of *equivocation*: "The use of words, phrases, or gestures having more than one meaning in order to conceal information which a questioner has no strict right to know. It is permissible to equivocate (have a broad mental reservation) in some circumstances. (2) A lie, i.e., a statement of untruth.

239

Lying is intrinsically wrong. A lie told in joking, evident as such, is not wrong."

The Catholic approach is nonsensical because it would prohibit a lie to save another's life. Additional questions arise: Who has a "right" to elicit information from another, except in a parent-child relationship, a court proceeding, or other custodial relationships? What "circumstances" allow skirting the truth? Why is lying intrinsically wrong when it harms no one else, especially when it may benefit either or both parties without harm to either?

When can we ethically break a promise to another or breach a contract? When it doesn't physically or monetarily harm the other party. When can we justify taking or damaging another's property? When it harms no one else, which is likely never. When is euthanasia justified? When it harms no one else without cognizant consent, which means it is justified when the recipient consents (and is mentally competent to consent) or is a hopeless vegetable. Harming no one else does not condemn suicide. The competent adult (would a competent adult contemplate suicide?) should be allowed to risk harm to himself as he chooses, no matter the danger of activities ranging from alligator-wrestling to hang-gliding. Suicide would include preplanned and voluntary euthanasia, such as with a living will. Of course, 99 percent of competent adults would never consider an act as foolish as suicide, alligator-wrestling, or driving in Los Angeles traffic. Harming no one else is a do-it-yourself system of freedom that virtually anyone can easily understand and follow.

Capital punishment would no longer be allowed under the prohibition against harming another. Instead, the ultimate punishment would be life in prison. Execution of murderers and prison itself is primarily for revenge and deterrence, dropping society to the moral level of the murderer. Can we eventually rise above "an eye for an eye and a tooth for tooth"? Outlawing capital punishment would greatly simplify and streamline the criminal justice system and save enormous sums of money. Automatic death penalty appeals keep murderers and other capital criminals in limbo for an average of ten years and treats offenders so inefficiently (and unequally by race) that the odds of execution for murder is one in twenty-five hundred. Additionally, it's far less expensive to keep a murderer in prison for life than pay lawyers to pursue interminable appeals.

Have you checked out lawyer's fees recently? They add up much faster than keeping someone in prison for an average of $32,000 a year in 2015, or $72 a day. Attorney's fees range between $255 and $520 an hour, and death row appeals cost an average of $700,000 more than similar cases without the death penalty. The death penalty makes no sense unless our primary motivation is revenge.

How does harming no one else as a system of ethics work in concrete situations, illustrated by some of the ethical issues of our time: abortion, poverty, and the war on drugs?

The Ethics of Abortion

Abortion is a muddied-up moral issue that boils down to this: When is the mother's right to autonomy over her body overridden by the life of what would otherwise be a legal person in a few months? Comprehensive polls by Kaiser, Pew, Reuters, Politico, and Gallup in 2018 found that half of Americans believe "abortions should only be legal under certain circumstances," though the circumstances are unclear.

The respective positions on abortion and when life begins were summed up by Donald Kaul, a columnist for the *Des Moines Register*: "On one hand we have those who believe it [life] begins at the moment of conception and that your average fetus will probably become Albert Einstein, given half a chance. At the other extreme there are those who believe life begins at birth and before that, an unborn fetus deserves all the consideration generally reserved for pet rocks."

Roe v. Wade marks the point of theoretical viability of the fetus and prohibits abortion from the beginning of the third trimester. However, the concept of viability is one the Supreme Court pulled out of a hat with no legal precedent; neither does the concept have a medical basis (though it does have a psychological basis). Even a normally delivered and healthy baby isn't viable; without constant attention a newborn would die in a few days. Physical milestones such as a heartbeat or brain waves would be more logically supportable than viability. However, we routinely distinguish between a miscarriage and a stillbirth on the basis of the age of the fetus. The Supreme Court in *Roe v. Wade* chose an expedient middle ground it thought would solve the problem. It hasn't.

A 2018 Gallup poll found that 60 percent of Americans support abortions in the first three months; 28 percent support abortion from the third to the sixth month, and 13 percent after six months. If we are unsure when human life begins, shouldn't ethics require that we err on the side of life? Isn't the touchstone of civilization the right of each of us to develop into the best we can be without our lives being cut short without our consent or for the convenience of others?

It appears inconsistent to argue that an aborted twenty-six-week-old fetus is not a human being while a baby born prematurely after twenty-six weeks is a human being. The real question is whether the twenty-six-week unborn fetus should be considered a legal person with rights like the rest of us; it's certainly a human being though unborn. We should then consider the relative moral rights of the unborn human being and its mother and whether those rights should differ, depending on the circumstances under which the mother becomes pregnant.

Most of us feel that the person with the greatest life expectancy should first be saved from a sinking ship. Why do we reverse the presumption with regard to abortion? Why do we prefer to save the life of a mother, with between forty and sixty years of life expectancy, instead of the fetus, with eighty years of life expectancy?

* * *

Feminist arguments fall on both sides of the abortion divide. Early feminists, such as Susan B. Anthony, Elizabeth Cady Stanton, and Margaret Sanger, the founder of Planned Parenthood, were against abortion. More recently, a president-elect of the National Organization for Women remarked, "We don't favor abortion. We're in favor of women being able to make the choice. That's what liberating is all about." Feminists for Life International, headquartered in Ireland and the U.S., supports criminalization of all abortions, even to save the life of the mother. The U.S. organization, which boasts 26,000 members, takes the position that abortion "allows men to continue to be virtually free of responsibility for the results of their sexual activity." The point is well taken. Men have an equal responsibility to harm no one else, and failing to support their children constitutes harm.

A 2018 Gallup poll found that 55 percent of Americans disapproved of abortion for any financial reason, even if a teenager would otherwise have to drop out of school or was "abandoned by her partner." A large majority disapproved of abortion to prevent interruption of a career, rising to almost 90 percent disapproval as "repeated" birth control. Yet, most abortions (86 percent) are by single women; 75 percent live at or below the poverty line. In 2014 it cost an average of $233,000 to raise a child, an almost impossible sum for a poor pregnant single mother-to-be.

The *Los Angeles Times* published a letter to the editor from a female gynecologist that read in part, "All too frequently I have had the following conversation with my female patients: 'Are you sexually active?' 'Yes.' 'Are you using any form of birth control?' 'No.' 'Do you want to get pregnant at this time?' 'No.' 'Then why aren't you using anything?' 'I don't know.' . . . I'm angered with women who are so irresponsible with their bodies that they use abortion as a form of birth control. How hard is it to get a condom . . .?"

With few exceptions, pregnancy is avoidable. Only about 1.5 percent of abortions result from rape or incest. If a person, male or female, chooses to avoid responsibility for birth control when no child is wanted from sex, the ethical answer would not appear to be an abortion. The first ethical question is therefore whether the convenience of the mother, no matter her right to bodily autonomy, is moral justification for the termination of a pregnancy.

* * *

The "It's my body" justification for abortion seems peculiarly illogical when "It's my body" is no defense to the use of illegal drugs, which have no implication for the life or death of a potential human being, unless the drug user is a pregnant female. In other words, based on a harm-no-one-else analysis, abortion harms "someone" else or "someone else with certainty," while illegal drug use does not. The second fallacy of the "It's my body" argument is that the fetus is not the body of the mother but something separate and distinguishable from her body. It is a viable argument that a woman can decide whether to cut off her own finger, for that is clearly her body; the fetus, however, is not, but is only a temporary parasite within her body, which she had equal responsibility in placing there. Of course, historically, many if not most males have borne no responsibility whatsoever.

Courts are grappling with whether drug use during pregnancy constitutes child abuse or assault of the fetus. Research proves that a pregnant woman's use of certain drugs, including tobacco and alcohol, may have severe consequences for the developing fetus and, on average, doubles the rate of stillbirths. When harm is inflicted on another, does it make any difference whether the harm-creating mechanism may be legally bought or sold? And if it's legal to abort an unborn child, how can it be illegal to inflict a lesser harm?

Proponents point out that if a pregnant woman is held responsible for damage to the fetus, the door opens to regulate her every move, shades of *The Handmaiden's Tale* and *Stepford Wives*. This "slippery slope" argument reasons that if the state can forbid drug use during pregnancy then it can dictate what a pregnant woman may eat or drink, the number of hours she may work, and the conditions under which sex is permitted. Most agree that imposition of criminal law sanctions against women using drugs is inappropriate and counterproductive because they will then avoid prenatal care, compounding the harm. The question remains whether it's appropriate to regulate the privacy of those who use drugs that harm themselves while drawing the line at regulating the privacy of those who use drugs that may harm others, though the other is an unborn child with no legal rights.

* * *

Effective contraception and universal sex education in schools would in all likelihood defuse the destructive debate surrounding abortion. According to a report by the National Academy of Sciences, "The inadequacy of current contraceptive methods contributes to the problems of unintended pregnancy, unwanted children and high rates of abortions. The stronger the desire to reduce abortion, the greater should be the investment to develop new methods of contraception." The report concluded that half of the abortions performed in the United States could be avoided if a broader range of contraceptives were available.

Most religions, however, oppose both birth control and sex education except for "just saying no" to sex. The Huffington Post reported in 2017 that states relying on abstinence-only programs had the highest incidence of teen pregnancy and births. California ended its abstinence-only program in 1995 when it found that it had no effect on the age when teens began having sex. It mandated sex education that was medically accurate, age-appropriate, and comprehensive, which by 2005 cut the teen pregnancy rate more than half, a phenomenal result because teen pregnancies are the ones that most often end in abortion.

Catholics, Baptists, and other fundamentalist religions are against abortion for any reason. A Catholic bishop said Governor Cuomo of New York was "in serious risk of going to hell" for supporting abortion rights. (The threat of hell is perhaps less of a threat after Pope Francis said in 2018 that bad souls simply disappear. Word spread that hell no longer exists, but the pope walked it back, perhaps because almost two-thirds of us still believe in hell.)

Judaism holds that a fetus is not human life because the Talmud distinguishes between actual and potential life. The Evangelical Lutheran Church in America, the Presbyterian Church-USA, the United Methodist Church, and the Episcopal Church condone abortion in certain circumstances, though each has anti-abortion factions.

A 2017 poll by the Pew Research Center resulted in the following findings:

- Seven in ten white evangelical Protestants (70 percent) think abortion should be illegal in all or most cases.

- In contrast, 80 percent of religiously unaffiliated Americans say abortion should be legal in all or most cases, as do two-thirds of white mainline Protestants (67 percent).

- Black Protestants and Catholics are somewhat more divided. Among black Protestants, 55 percent say abortion should be legal in all or most cases, while 41 percent say it should be illegal. Among Catholics, 53 percent say abortion should be legal in all or most cases, and 44 percent say it should be illegal.

Our society believes in killing. Police may shoot to kill; capital punishment is legal in most states (thirty-one of fifty, plus the federal government and the military); war is waged with little thought of consequences to civilians; each cut in a social program to feed the homeless or provide health care may cause death. However, we often have a choice whether to participate in crime or war when there's no draft, or when the possibility of raising money necessary for food or a transplant exists. The fetus has no say-so at all; to argue that a child would rather be aborted than born into poverty, without consulting the child, would appear illogical. Naturally the fetus cannot be consulted, yet if any fetus could respond, it seems a fair assumption that few would choose oblivion.

Of course, the abortion debate asks whether the fetus is a lump of flesh without rights or a legal person with rights of due process, which would require no harm without consent or an opportunity to be heard, which would make the whole question moot. How the answer to this question can depend on the circumstances by which the mother became pregnant is unclear. The circumstances of conception make no difference to the victim of an abortion, unless we return to the years where a bastard was ostracized by society. For example, the late blues singer Ethel Waters was the product of the rape of her twelve-year-old mother. She and others were grateful she was not aborted. Or is this irrelevant?

For those who assert that severe health defects should justify abortion, there is Beethoven, the fourth child of a syphilitic father and consumptive mother, with two tubercular sisters during a period when tuberculosis was a dread disease. How many of the 800,000 aborted fetuses in this country would fall into the prodigy category, or is it relevant? If it is not relevant or important, why not? To justify abortion these questions should be answered, instead of evaded or ignored. Of course, we'll never know; does this mean it makes no difference and is this a sufficient answer?

The language of abortion is similar to the terms used by slave owners in the early 1800s. Southerners weren't pro-slavery because anyone was free to own or not own slaves. Southerners were pro-choice on slavery. By this logic no one can be either pro-slavery or pro-abortion because no one has ever proposed that Southerners be required to own slaves any more than anyone has advocated that all pregnant women be required to have an abortion. Southerners asked, Why don't those Northerners leave us alone and mind their own business instead of imposing their druthers on us; how many Northerners would be willing to support and feed slaves if they were freed? Similarly, one argument is that those opposed to abortion must be prepared to adopt the resulting child when the mother, for her personal convenience, would rather have an abortion. As Leo Tolstoy, the inspiration for the nonviolent philosophies of Gandhi and Martin Luther King, wrote in his diary in 1852, "It is true that slavery is an evil, but an extremely convenient evil." Abortion is similarly an evil of convenience.

The language in the abortion debate is sanitized; the killing of the fetus/child is called termination of pregnancy; a human life becomes a fetus or potential life; the man or woman doing the killing is called a doctor, or provider. What does the right to choose mean; that is to say, what is being chosen? Is there an answer other than the death of an unborn child? How can a human being choose the death of another human being without that human being's consent in a society where consent to physical injury is illegal and imposes civil liability? Why do pictures of an aborted fetus enrage pro-abortionists when the pictures accurately portray exactly what occurs in an abortion? If abortion is morally neutral, what difference does it make how many abortions have been performed each year or whether abortion is routinely used for birth control? Why is a confessed murderer entitled to a jury while an innocent and unborn child may be "terminated" or killed on the whim of the mother? Why does the potential father have no legal interest in the question of whether to abort when the father is responsible for eighteen years of child support upon a child's birth? Only by denying the existence of human life can these questions be answered, and even then, any answer is unsatisfactory.

We do, however, distinguish how we feel about the death of a fetus. An early death is called a miscarriage, which for many is relatively atraumatic. A later death is called stillbirth, which most potential mothers feel more intensely. This distinction is logical based on fetal development. At the moment of conception, the zygote, a single egg and sperm, is barely visible to the naked eye, about the size of the period at the end of this sentence. After one month the fetus is the size of a quarter, and by the third month the size of a large hen egg. Half the weight of the fetus is gained the last six to eight weeks. However, the fetus is reactive from the fourth month, moving when startled by noise and turning away when a light is shined on the mother's stomach. Most abortions occur before the end of the first trimester, perhaps justified by the lack of reactivity until the beginning of the fourth month. By the sixth month the fetus responds to music, soothed by ballads and agitated by hard rock, with the ability to grin, grimace, and frown. Except for weight, a third-trimester fetus is almost indistinguishable from a newborn child, a fact recognized by most abortion advocates who agree that late-term abortions should not be performed after six months. However, it's difficult to draw the line between the one hundred seventy-ninth day and the one hundred eightieth day. It's also difficult to justify abortion after reactiveness begins in the fourth month. How can abortion be moral on one day and not on the next, when there's no significant difference in reactiveness?

Assuming a fetus is not a sentient being, then is the killing of any nonsentient human life equally acceptable? For example, if my father is senile with Alzheimer's disease, bed-ridden, and an inconvenient burden, what difference is there between killing that nonsentient being and a nonsentient fetus? One clear distinction is that the fetus has a fruitful life expectancy of eighty years, while the father has a maximum life expectancy of a few months while basically unconscious. Logically then, it should be less immoral to kill the father than to kill the fetus.

I suggest the following as a solution to the current abortion quagmire, which technology, early and continuous sex education, and freely available and effective birth control will hopefully resolve. Almost half of us believe abortion is immoral but most also believe a woman should be able to choose whether to have an abortion during the first three months of pregnancy. We can distinguish between legality and morality. Most of us agree that "I personally feel that abortion is morally wrong, but I also feel that whether or not to have an abortion is a decision that has to be made by every woman for herself." Accordingly, 62 percent opposed a constitutional amendment banning abortion. We appear internally confused on abortion, perhaps for the first time in our history having a majority believing an act to be immoral but opposing *criminal* sanctions. The distinction between criminal sanctions and civil remedies is crucial but has never, to my knowledge, been analyzed in connection with the abortion debate.

We should reject criminal justice sanctions, which is the specter that likely provides the most support for the status quo on abortion. Instead, abortion should be reserved as a civil law question, so that any person directly impacted by an abortion can bring a civil suit for damages. As in any civil case, damages would only be recoverable by an immediate relative, someone with a direct legal interest in the question.

Those who have no direct personal interest would be prohibited from harassing pregnant mothers and abortion clinics, but any affected person, whether the potential father or other close relative, should be allowed to sue for damages caused to them, if any, by the aborting of their soon to be offspring or relative. Of course, since 75 percent of women who abort are too poor to raise a child, which is why they obtain an abortion in the first place, the possibility of a civil damage recovery is remote at best. Still, the specter of the criminal justice system should be removed from the equation.

This is only a temporary solution. Because abortion harms another, whether the other is called a fetus or human being, and is thus immoral in the ultimate sense of what morality is all about, a compromise is necessary until we as a species can become more civilized and caring toward our offspring, potential and actual, who are all human beings. Birth control should be removed from the list of religious prohibitions, allowing the shy and the rest of society to practice prevention when no child is wanted from sex. The bottom line of abortion is that it harms someone else and is thus immoral. Failure to use birth control when no child is sought lacks personal responsibility; nor is there any justification in harming another for the convenience of the irresponsible.

Religion and Poverty

Although the Bible describes the love of money as the root of all evil (not an unreasonable conclusion), religion and money, tithes and offerings, are inseparable. Tithes and tithing are mentioned thirty-seven times in the Bible. According to the Lilly Family School of Philanthropy at the University of Indiana, American donations to religious organizations totaled more than $120 billion in 2016, amounting to a third of all charitable donations and twice as much as we gave to the next highest category, education. None of the world's thousands of churches reveal how much they use to support the poor, but the figure is obviously a tiny percentage or it would be publicized. Instead, these billions aren't used to feed and clothe the poor because suffering in this life is not only considered unimportant, but it is encouraged by many religions. Religion is in the business of saving souls and not physical bodies.

The billions of dollars collected by religions instead went to support religious leaders and televangelist jets, and to build magnificent edifices, which do as much to glorify the particular religion and its leaders as to glorify its God. According to the hunger-relief charity Feeding America, 42 million Americans are hungry at this very moment, one of every seven of us. Our hungry are fed by our two hundred food banks and sixty thousand food pantries, and include a fourth of our military families.

One of every five human beings in the world, or well over a billion people, suffers from malnutrition, poor health, or disease. Half of the world's child mortality rate is attributable to hunger that leads to disease and poor health. In Arizona alone fifty thousand people go to bed hungry every night; thirty thousand of these are children. A fourth of the hungry are over age sixty, with two thirds choosing between food and paying utilities. Almost half are diabetic, and more than half must choose between buying food or medicine.

A 2010 Gallup poll found a strong correlation between religiosity and poverty without exploring why this might be true. Perhaps it's because the Bible tells us the poor are always with us, a position espoused by Mother Theresa, who concluded that the poor should therefore stay poor.

Or perhaps devout religion helps preserve the state, as Napoleon Bonaparte (1769–1821) seems to have believed. The Corsican emperor of France is quoted by several biographers as saying, "Religion is excellent stuff for keeping common people quiet."

Or there's the study by Dr. Tom Rees in the *Journal of Religion and Society* (Vol. 11), analyzing "data from over 50 countries representing a wide range of religions, wealth, and social structures." He used income inequality to measure the degree of personal insecurity faced by people in those countries. The findings may explain why conventional theories about the impact of religion have always fallen short. Conventional theories on why religiosity varies so widely from place to place claim that modernization leads to loss of faith, or that countries interfering with religion cause disenchantment with religion. However, neither theory explains the differences among wealthy countries. Dr. Rees's analysis shows a high correlation between personal insecurity and countries that are more religious than others. Indeed, personal insecurity is the single most important factor in predicting national variations in religiosity. "This is because inequality is associated with a range of social problems that combine to make people feel insecure and in need of the comfort offered by religion," suggests Dr. Rees. He also confirmed that "more religious nations have more indicators of social disharmony, with lower life expectancy, higher infant mortality, higher murder rates, more corruption, and a higher number of abortions. They also scored worse on the Global Peace index, that is, they are less peaceful both internally and in their external relations. The research showed that nations with high levels of belief in God, Hell and the Devil ('passionate dualism') have higher murder rates." The combined effects of personal insecurity, modernization, and freedom of religion explain most of the differences between countries. For the first time, we have a comprehensive theory of national religiosity, explaining religiousness in countries as diverse as India and Germany.

Most of the hungry live in Catholic and other fundamentalist countries: Central America, South America, Asia, and Africa. In *Prosperity and Poverty: The Compassionate Use of Resources in a World of Scarcity,* Calvin Beisner concludes that real Christian concern about poverty could easily solve the problem. Using a rough estimate of the income of U.S. church members, one percent of their income, which is only one-tenth of a tithe, would be sufficient to eliminate poverty worldwide. In Phoenix, when the homeless seek places to sleep, accommodations are provided by state and city tax money. The churches contribute little, though church buildings are used only a fraction of the time and few are used at night.

The average tithe is 1.9 percent, or less than a fifth of the amount mandated by the Bible. Protestants give the bulk of this percentage while Catholics average 0.9 percent. Jews give an average of 1.5 percent. Islam requires a 2.5 percent tithe as alms for the poor. The reasons for giving vary widely. One parishioner was told by his priest that "God will be better to you if you give more." Rev. Andrew Greeley estimated that U.S. Catholics withhold billions of dollars in donations yearly to protest what they view as problems within the church ranging from papal authority and birth control to corruption and pedophilia. By 2019 Pew Research found that 31 percent of Catholics rated the clergy's honesty highly, a steep drop from 49 percent in 2017. Catholic confidence in organized religion suffered an eight-point drop in two years, down to 44 percent in 2019.

Theology professor James Cone, of the Union Theological Seminary in New York, was interviewed by *USA Today* when he was honored at the Howard University divinity school's conference on black theology. Professor Cone was asked, "Why are churches so silent in the face of social chaos?" He answered, "With few exceptions, churches are primarily focusing on their own survival, building bigger churches and holding fund-raisers for their pastors." Catholic schools are no longer able to subsidize their poorer students because, according to the president of the Arizona Council for Academic Education, "We don't have the resources to help the poor."

The Yoga Bhajan, leader to three million of the world's fifteen million Sikhs, described the relationship between money and religion: "Religious men became very corrupt because we religious men have to go and get money from you. We compromise for a better congregation, to attract rich people." Or as L. Ron Hubbard, founder of Scientology, said, "If you want to get rich, you start a religion." Or even better, start a religion for insecure Hollywood stars and become uber-rich.

* * *

The inefficiency with which religious institutions

spend their income is on a par with that of governments; taxes and tithes both get lost in the bureaucratic shuffle. The difference is that it's impossible to obtain even a general accounting of how religious contributions are spent. The percentage of church income that reaches the poor and needy is minute. Is it unfair to point out that little or nothing goes from churches to the "less fortunate" and that church buildings, such as the Vatican, are expensive to maintain? Vatican II recognized that Vatican finances are a public relations disaster and acknowledged the following facts: Vatican assets in 1965 (excluding works of art and real estate, the value of which is astronomical) equaled the wealth of the French government and were five times the British reserve. Vatican funds were deposited in the Bank of the Holy Spirit, which is fully invested. Cardinals are chauffeured around Rome, where most Italians ride scooters or walk. The Catholic palace in Karachi is a particular affront to the local poor.

The sources of Vatican wealth include the Inquisitions and the Crusades, which for hundreds of years drained the resources of poor church members. In all wars until the 1800s the booty of the losers was split between the church and the state. Charlemagne required all conquered peoples to join the church or die. Tithes were compulsory. Upon the death of Charlemagne in 814, the pope inherited the wealth of the empire. After Pope John XXII was elected in 1316, he confiscated a fortune valued at forty times the wealth of France. The French government was unable to raise 400,000 florins to ransom King John; Pope John XXII died worth twenty-five million florins. During the Middle Ages, in addition to penances, indulgences, and confiscations, the church levied taxes heavier than those imposed by kings. Franciscans were burned during the Inquisitions for wearing their frock, which symbolized vows of poverty.

The leaders of all major religions are used to posh living. Protecting church property and Christian missionaries has justified Western imperialism, making Easterners suspicious of Western missionaries and their wealth. Yet reform is difficult; Vatican II's primary recommendation was that priests and nuns wear simple costumes to avoid the appearance of wealth.

The Church of Jesus Christ of Latter-day Saints is a diversified corporation engaged in many businesses, including insurance, broadcasting, publishing, satellite communications, schools, property development, department stores, hotels, and a new $1.5 billion mall in downtown Salt Lake City where the prophet cut the ribbon and exclaimed, "Let's go shopping." Mormons tithed (as of 2010) $33 billion yearly, and church-owned business generated about $15 billion. This would place the church seventy-ninth on the Fortune 500 list, ahead of American Express, Coca-Cola, Time Warner, and General Dynamics.

It is one of the largest landowners in the country, with holdings in all fifty states, all tax-exempt. It has television and radio stations in many major cities. Its worldwide missionary program is second only to the Roman Catholic Church, which has about 150,000 missionaries to the Mormon's 71,000. The church regards accounting for its expenditures as a sacrilege, as do all churches, succinctly described in advice given to the church's first counselor, President Ezra Taft Benson, by his father, Gordon B. Hinckley:

> "He reminded me that mine is the God-given obligation to pay my tithes and offerings. When I do so, that which I give is no longer mine. It belongs to the Lord to whom I consecrate it. What the authorities of the church do with it need not concern me. They are answerable to the Lord, who will require an accounting at their hands."

Mormons, to remain in good standing, must swear they have tithed (a full 10 percent of their income) or if not, state the percentage and vow to hit 10 percent soon. They are otherwise excluded from temples and certain benefits. All churches say, "Trust us with your money. We're infallible." The Mormon church goes the extra mile to obtain new members by offering interest-free loans to Tongan converts.

* * *

In 1989 Jim Bakker, the televangelist preacher, was convicted of twenty-four counts of fraud and conspiracy, sentenced to forty-five years in prison, and fined $500,000 for swindling $3.7 million from his followers. One victim was Jessica Hahn, who was paid $279,000 for keeping quiet about her rape by Bakker. Bakker's forty-five-year sentence was reduced to eight years, and he was paroled in 1994. By 2003 Jim Bakker had remarried and was again preaching "prosperity theology," founded on the premise that "God wants you to be rich." Viewers give Mr. Bakker money because he promises they will become rich if they do. His fellow televangelists are not amused. Jerry Falwell called Bakker "the greatest scab and cancer on the face of Christianity in 2,000 years of church history" and Jimmy Swaggart told Larry King that Jim Bakker was a "cancer in the body of Christ." By 2019 Jim Bakker was one of the world's richest ex-cons.

In 2015 John Oliver exposed televangelists who fleece their flocks for millions of dollars, including televangelist Mike Murdock, who instructs those deep in credit card debt to pony up $1,000 for the Murdock ministry; that contribution, he promises, will sow a seed and God will wipe out the donor's credit card debt. Televangelist Kenneth Copeland convinced Bonnie Parker to forgo treatment for cancer and promised that if she would instead donate the money to Copeland's church her cancer would be cured. She donated and died. The Copelands live in a $6.3 million mansion, a tax-free parsonage.

The 2017 tax reform act, according to *Salon* magazine, effectively created a way to launder dark money through churches. The repeal of the Johnson Amendment (which prohibited church endorsements of political candidates) allows the lauding of political candidates from the pulpit. This could "allow a big political donor who wants to make a contribution to give to a church, which could then endorse a candidate and engage in electioneering."

CNBC reported in 2018 that religious frauds are the hardest to combat, totaling billions of dollars yearly. For example, Ephron Taylor fleeced $16 million from church members in forty-three states by preaching prosperity gospel and is now serving a nineteen-year prison sentence. Bernie Madoff preyed on Jewish communities in Florida and New York, bilking them of almost $20 billion. These scams are powerful because they harness the magnetism of religion, which is faith, belief in something for which there is no objective evidence. Securities officials believe the fraud is far greater than the cases reported, because many people would rather take their losses then admit gullibility. Officials recommend wariness of "Christian financial planners," the use of religion to obtain business, new church members who spring from nowhere with sure-fire investments, and claims that "religiously based investments are not regulated by state laws."

The IRS has audited only two churches in its entire history. In 2018 Congress imposed severe limitations on when the IRS is allowed to audit a church, according to the IRS website: "The IRS may begin a church tax inquiry only if an appropriate high-level Treasury official reasonably believes, on the basis of facts and circumstances recorded in writing, that an organization claiming to be a church or convention or association of churches may not qualify for exemption, may be carrying on an unrelated trade or business (within the meaning of IRC § 513), may otherwise be engaged in taxable activities or may have entered into an IRC § 4958 excess benefit transaction with a disqualified person." Fraud is not an issue.

The Religious Prohibition Against Birth Control

The greatest burden imposed on women by many religions is the prohibition against birth control. The condemnation of sex except for procreation is a doctrine central to Catholicism, Mormonism, many Protestant denominations, and Islam, and its impact on women and the world at large is enormous. *The Catholic Word Book* calls contraception an unnatural act, as "against the order of nature." Donor artificial insemination is prohibited, as described in *The Catholic Word Book:* "In view of the principle that procreation should result only from marital intercourse, donor insemination is not permissible. The use of legitimate artificial means to further the fruitfulness of marital intercourse is permissible."

According to a 2016 *Scientific American* article the current 1.2 billion population of Africa, our poorest continent, will increase to between 3 billion and 6 billion mostly destitute folks by 2100. This is because men's control over women extends to women's ability to obtain and use birth control and to determine whether to bear children and how many. *Scientific American* fails to note that these two reasons, male dominance and prohibitions against birth control, are a mainstay of the vast majority of all religions. Having lived in 170 of the world's countries (out of 193 in the United Nations) as a travel writer, I found that Africa is by far the most religious continent, dominated by fundamentalist Islam and Christianity. Most Africans I've met believe everything said in the Bible or Quran; men rule, and women do what they're told. By 2018 some small progress had been made, illustrated by the lowering of fertility rates in Mauritius from 6 to 1.5 children per couple and in Tunisia from 7 to 2.

World population increases by 90 million people per year and continues to spiral upward. The United Nations and private demographers predict geometric population increases reaching a catastrophic level within thirty years, unless worldwide family planning is strengthened. Of course, similar catastrophes have been predicted for centuries. These enormous increases are predicted in third world countries where religion dominates, usually Catholic, Muslim, or Hindu.

The prohibition against birth control has made Islam the world's fastest-growing religion, with 1.8 billion adherents, a fourth of the world's population, while a sixth is irreligious. The average Islamic woman bears six children, and if the rate continues, Muslims will constitute the world's largest religion in thirty to forty years, leaving Christianity in the rearview window.

Bangladesh is about half the size of Arizona, has an estimated (who really knows?) population of 166 million people projected to increase to over 200 million by 2050, and is obviously losing its battle to fight the population explosion, which lengthens its lead as the most densely populated country in the world and one of the most devout Islamic countries. K. T. Hosain, a Dhaka University social scientist, says, "There is not a ghost of a chance that this [population reduction] target can be achieved in a poor, largely rural and traditional society bound by Islamic mores against artificial birth control measures." Females are ostracized if they practice birth control.

The prohibition against birth control is self-serving for any religion. The best way for a religion to grow is to enjoin birth control, baptize infants, and perpetuate the passage of the family religion from generation to generation, in perpetuity. Use of birth control by a woman requires excommunication from the male-dominated religion she was raised to serve. This keeps women (and their children) in poverty.

The number of babies born to single mothers in the United States rose from 3.8 percent in 1951 to 40 percent in 2018, with 70 percent of black mothers unmarried; most children of single mothers are raised in poverty. Over one million unmarried teenage girls become pregnant in the United States each year while many conservative religions oppose sex education in public schools. The reason our public policy continues to avoid talking about the problem is simple, organized religion. Pat Robertson illustrated the fundamentalist attitude toward sexual equality for women in a fund-raising letter opposing the Iowa equal rights amendment, citing a "secret feminist agenda" that is "not about equal rights for women. It is about a socialist, anti-family political movement that encourages women to leave their husbands, kill their children, practice witchcraft, destroy capitalism and become lesbians." The Public Religion Research Institute found in 2015 that "Three-quarters (75%) of millennials favor teaching comprehensive sex education in public schools, while 21% are opposed. Support for this policy cuts across all racial, ethnic, and religious groups." The study also found that "More than two-thirds (67%) of millennials say that emphasizing safe sexual practices and birth control is a better way to prevent unintended pregnancy than emphasizing abstinence from sex (23%). There is general agreement across racial and ethnic lines on this question. White evangelical Protestant millennials stand apart from other millennials, with half (50%) favoring an emphasis on birth control, compared to 40% favoring an emphasis on abstinence, and eight percent in favor of emphasizing both."

Almost all organized religions oppose sex education in schools and effective birth control, our two best chances to substantially lower the abortion rate in the United States. Yet they almost all oppose abortion. This is called hypocrisy.

An Ethical Response to Illegal Drugs

The traditional purpose of government is to protect its citizens from harm. The seriousness of a crime is judged by the harm caused to the victim. Because murder causes more harm than burglary, the sentence for murder is longer and more severe. For a narrow class of "moral" crimes, however, the criminal justice system dispenses with this logic and punishes those who primarily harm themselves and only incidentally, if at all, harm others. These are commonly called victimless crimes.

Victimless "moral" crimes include the use, possession, and sale of illegal drugs. The other main categories are gambling, pornography, and prostitution. Excluded from the victimless-crime category would be drugs sold to minors or ingested by pregnant women, which either harm a soon-to-be person or harm a minor who is considered unable to legally make these decisions.

Crimes without victims raise serious questions of ethics and the involvement of the criminal justice system. To fully understand the appropriateness of criminalizing victimless behavior requires the consideration of the following eight factors:

(1) the relative harms of victimless behaviors

(2) the reasons people "commit" victimless crimes

(3) the costs of and our ability to prevent or punish victimless behavior

(4) the special status of minors

(5) how valuable we consider privacy, liberty, and freedom from interference by government

(6) the ethical justification for imprisoning an individual

(7) the source of "moral" crimes without victims

(8) the impact if victimless crimes were legalized.

These eight factors, as they relate to illegal drugs and other victimless crimes, are explored in this and subsequent chapters.

The Relative Harms of Illegal and Legal Drugs

Americans are as well-educated about drugs as we are about geography and history. Few of us know that the most dangerous drug in the world is tobacco. The second most dangerous drug is alcohol. According to the National Institutes of Health: "An estimated 88,000 people (approximately 62,000 men and 26,000 women) die from alcohol-related causes annually, making alcohol the third leading preventable cause of death in the United States. The first is tobacco, and the second is poor diet and physical inactivity."

Camus said, "Every ambiguity, every misunderstanding, leads to death; clear language and simple words are the only salvation from this death." The drug problem in the United States is largely due to our ignorance about drugs and our obfuscation of their relative effects and dangers. Instead of distinguishing between our drugs, we lump them together and make most either illegal or obtainable by prescription only, on the assumption that the government must make drug decisions for its adults. No other country in the world has as many illegal and "prescription only" drugs as the United States. When it comes to drugs we are among the most paternalistic nations in the world.

Any drug is dangerous if too much is consumed, or if the drug is impure, whether the drug is aspirin, alcohol, or heroin. Conversely, few drugs (other than pure poison) used in moderation are dangerous to the user, with the exception of highly addicting drugs such as methamphetamine, opioids, tobacco, alcohol, cocaine, and, when available in relatively pure dosages, morphine, opium, and heroin. No drug is completely harmless. The potential for harm depends on the dosage and purity.

Drugs generally fall into eight broad and unscientific categories:

- Narcotics relieve pain and reduce coughing

and diarrhea when used in moderation. Only opiates are properly classified as narcotics. The two primary narcotics are morphine and codeine produced from opium and the semi-synthetics used by the health profession. All narcotics produce euphoria, and all are physically addictive.

- Central nervous system depressants create tolerance resulting in dependence. Marijuana is a central nervous system depressant.

- Sedatives and hypnotics calm the user, induce sleep, and are physically addictive. They are primarily used to treat insomnia (19 million prescriptions a year), anxiety, and seizures. Sedatives account for 20 percent of our prescription drugs. Barbiturates are dangerous because the dose for sedation is only a fraction less than the amount that causes a coma or death. Approximately three thousand deaths result yearly from overdoses of barbiturates in the U.S., with 42 percent classified as suicides and the rest accidental.

- Anti-anxiety drugs and minor tranquilizers cause psychological dependence.

- Ethanol and alcohol are the second most widely used and physically addictive drugs.

- Anesthetics are rarely used illegally, except for cocaine, which overlaps many general drug categories; anesthetics are physically addictive.

- Stimulants of the central nervous system include amphetamines and cocaine (also an anesthetic), originating from plants and synthetics; they are psychologically addictive. Coffee, tea, chocolate, and caffeine are the most widely used "soft" drugs and constitute central nervous system stimulants.

- Nicotine is a physically addictive central nervous system stimulant derived from tobacco and, together with crack and ice, the most addictive substance known.

An excessive dosage of any drug results in sleep, unconsciousness, or death. No drug is either demon or innocent; everything depends on the user, the dosage, and the environment of use. Compare the effects of alcohol at social gatherings, 90 percent of which feature alcohol; some people are boisterous, others passive, a few aggressive, some sleepy, a few amorous, and many change little. Every other drug acts similarly; its effect depends on the personality of the individual, the amount consumed, the social setting, and the user's interaction with others.

Dangerous, bizarre, antisocial, and crazy behavior by a drug user is unrelated to the drug used (with the exception of hallucinogens, which may frighten the user, resulting in injury) and is instead dependent on the personality of the user and the social setting. In other words, no drug changes the personality of the user to the extent that the user would commit a crime that he has no unintoxicated proclivity to commit. In this regard drugs are similar to hypnosis.

The real danger of drugs is excessive use. Dependence or addiction develops rapidly once a drug is used regularly at any dosage. The Catch-22 is that many people are ill equipped to restrict drug use to moderate levels. The extent of dependence, addiction, and craving varies according to individual physiognomy and physiology; the consequences of prolonged use depend on the drug. The number of people using drugs to excess, however, is relatively small in any society, except for alcohol and tobacco, our most dangerous drugs, which we appear to care little about.

The following list shows the generally accepted comparative levels of addictiveness for our favorite drugs, with 100 points constituting almost immediate physical addiction, based on how easy it is to become addicted and how hard it is to stop using each drug:

- Nicotine, crack, ice, glass **100**
- Crystal meth, Valium **92**

- Heroin **86**
- Crank (meth nasally) **83**
- Cocaine **74**
- Caffeine **73**
- Marijuana **24**
- LSD, Mescaline **20**

Tobacco is the number-one cause of premature death in the United States and the world. It is the deadliest known carcinogen. According to the USDA, "tobacco kills more than AIDS, legal drugs, illegal drugs, road accidents, murder, and suicide combined." Ninety percent of tobacco users are hopelessly addicted, and 6 percent of these die every year.

American health costs from smoking reached $300 billion in 2018. On average, smokers die ten years earlier than nonsmokers. Cigarette smoking is responsible for more than 480,000 deaths per year in the United States, including over 41,000 deaths resulting from secondhand smoke. Worldwide, tobacco use causes nearly 6 million deaths per year, and current trends show that tobacco use will cause more than 8 million deaths annually by 2030.

A study of forty thousand Montreal women by McGill University showed that smoking is the most dangerous contributor to problematic birth outcomes, higher than use of cocaine, heroin, or alcohol. Compared to nonsmokers, almost 50 percent more female smokers miscarried.

Alcohol builds tolerances, causes traumatic withdrawal symptoms, and is widely used throughout the world for recreation, causing more deaths than any other drug except tobacco. Alcohol causes physical deterioration of the user and lowers the ability to function. Excessive use causes severe long-term effects, which vary substantially depending on the physiology of the user.

Depending on the definition used, there are 18 million alcoholics in the United States, one in twelve adults. Seven percent of alcohol users are hopelessly addicted, and 7 percent of these die yearly.

Amphetamines were synthesized in the United States beginning in 1933 and are widely used today, causing almost twice as many deaths as cocaine. Amphetamines are overprescribed and have little legitimate medical use, which is limited to treatment of hyperactive children and narcoleptics or epileptics. Their original use, similar to NoDoz, was to delay sleep for students and truck drivers, primarily with Benzedrine and inhalers. Psychological dependence rapidly follows. Dependency on amphetamines is similar to narcotic addiction, because the user becomes preoccupied with finding the next dose.

Marijuana causes calm and giddiness, prevents nausea, reduces blood pressure, stimulates appetite, kills pain, and suppresses convulsions. It has caused few confirmed deaths; those who smoke marijuana to excess go to sleep. Marijuana is a dangerous drug only when used while operating dangerous machinery, such as when driving a motor vehicle. Also, pot may impair brain function in younger users, who should obviously be kept far away from the drug. However, this is difficult because marijuana is easily available in every state. By 2018 ten states and the District of Columbia had legalized marijuana for recreational use and twenty-three had legalized it for medical use.

Marijuana is therapeutic for the nausea and vomiting caused by radio/chemotherapy. It reduces muscle spasms in multiple sclerosis patients, relieves the internal eye pressure induced by glaucoma, and combats asthma. A study by scientists at the University of Kentucky and Emory University noted that "marijuana is one of the potential nonopioid alternatives that can relieve pain at a relatively lower risk of addiction and virtually no risk of overdose." It found that laws allowing medical cannabis or recreational marijuana "have the potential to lower opioid prescribing for Medicaid enrollees, a high-risk population for chronic pain, opioid use disorder, and opioid overdose."

Why do we spend billions of dollars to imprison people for using our least dangerous drug, while the most dangerous and addictive drugs are legal and easily available to our children, with beer in the refrigerator and cigarettes on the coffee table?

The key question with any dependence, physical or psychological, is the extent of interference with life functions and self-development. Were we to think clearly about what is dangerous about drugs, whether legal or illegal, and the improper foods we eat, the bottom line is how they affect our lives. We are concerned about illegal drugs because they are addicting, though no more addicting than alcohol and tobacco. Addiction means we spend our time unproductively instead of doing those things we could otherwise be doing with family and friends, or to advance our career. This fact is important for understanding what is bad about any addiction. Addictions may shorten our lives, but the biggest problem is making us unproductive. When we are high, intoxicated, or ill from the side effects of drugs, we can't function to work or take care of ourselves and our families. We can't fulfill our human responsibilities. This is only true, however, if the addiction takes more of our time than can be justified by the resulting pleasure.

Why We Use and Adore Drugs

In his book, *Intoxication: Life in Pursuit of Artificial Paradise,* pharmacologist Ronald Siegel concludes that the pursuit of intoxication is the fourth basic human drive: "The drive to pursue intoxication is a common biological behavior throughout the animal kingdom. It's irrepressible, it's unstoppable, it has never gone away and never will go away. We might as well make the pursuit of it safe." Siegel opposes legalization of illegal drugs and long resisted the conclusion that intoxication is natural: "But everywhere I looked, in every species of animal, they were all doing what we're doing: getting high on plant drugs. They were going out of their normal feeding range just to get high." Bighorn sheep climb the sheerest cliffs not for food but to reach a lichen with mind-numbing narcotic properties. African elephants search for the fermented fruit of the Borassus tree and become stumbling drunk. Primates particularly go out of their way to ingest foul-tasting plants to get a buzz. According to Ethiopian tradition, coffee was discovered by goatherds around 900 C.E. when they noticed their animals leaping around after eating coffee beans. Cows and horses eat locoweed because of its hallucinogens, which may also kill them. Countless animal species ingest hallucinogenic mushrooms.

Siegel concludes that "trying to prevent drug use by outlawing it is like trying to treat AIDS by outlawing sex. Winning the war on drugs by eradicating nonmedical drug use is neither possible nor desirable."

James Schaefer, director of the Office of Alcohol and Drug Abuse Prevention at the University of Minnesota, suggests:

"If any society chose to reject alcohol, it would probably have other, more serious problems. There's the workplace, the homeplace and this third place where we talk, drink, and release ourselves from our everyday worries and troubles. A little bit of drinking goes a long way in terms of the health of the community. Without that outlet we'd have more fighting, violence, and civil strife. In Minnesota we recently passed stricter drunk driving laws. . .. When the cops started busting people, domestic violence increased. The heavy drinkers were staying at home. Bar sales went down, but package sales went up, as did spouse and child abuse. . .. In small-town America the bar is the gossip center, the center of social activity. Without the comer bar to go to, there would be more homicides and violence."

Because of their addictive properties, there will always be a demand for drugs such as cocaine, tobacco, and alcohol. A University of California-Irvine study found that addiction, learning, and intelligence involve identical processes at the cellular level. Biologists have long thought of brain function as a unit, but the UCI study discovered how individual cells respond to a cocaine fix:

"In a sense, the purpose of life is to activate our reward systems. Dopamine and the opioid peptides are transmitters in a very powerful control system based on a certain chemistry, and along come poppy seeds and coca leaves that have chemicals very similar to, or can pharmacologically interact with, these central systems. They go right in, do not pass go. So, if you're tapping into the natural, positive reinforcement systems, then to say that cocaine or amphetamines—or heroin or morphine—should be highly appealing is an understatement."

The researchers concluded that drug addiction, from a biological and medical standpoint, should be treated as a brain disease instead of a character flaw. A part of the brain called the *nucleus accumbens* orients us toward pleasure, including sex and drugs. Brain irregularities in this area appear to make some more susceptible to drug addiction, which is akin to self-medication. Some drugs may correct a genetically caused chemical imbalance. The chief of the Alcohol, Drug Abuse and Mental Health Administration estimated that from a third to a half of those addicted to a particular drug may have a genetic susceptibility, particularly alcoholics and users of cocaine. The gene affected is linked to receptors of dopamine, a brain chemical that creates the sensation of pleasure. Seventy-seven percent of alcoholics have the identified gene. A psychologist at a Pittsburgh clinic reported that "Many recovering drug abusers tell me, 'The moment I took my first drug, I felt normal for the first time.' It stabilizes them physiologically, at least in the short term." A psychiatrist at Harvard Medical School said, "We suspect that cocaine is a way certain people medicate themselves for depression." The head of the federal Alcohol, Drug Abuse and Mental Health Administration concluded that half of all alcoholics and 70 percent of those using illegal drugs to excess suffered from depression or severe anxiety before becoming addicted.

According to David Krogh, author of *Smoking: The Artificial Passion*, we use the "workplace drugs" of tobacco, Valium, and caffeine not so much for pleasurable sensation as to "get normal." Nicotine is a startling drug in that it relaxes tension but also acts as a mild stimulant for those feeling below par. Depressed people and schizophrenics are likely to smoke tobacco because it allows subtle mood regulation through self-medication.

Drugs lessen inhibitions and are a traditional means used by the male to seduce the female. Drugs provide gregariousness and social charm. Alcohol is more than socially acceptable—it's almost socially required. Drugs of any type are used to alleviate stress, which is what most if not all modern societies seem to provide in abundance.

How Effective Are Our Drug Policies

The U.S. has 4.4 percent of the world's population and 22 percent of its prisoners, mostly because of the war on drugs. Our drug stereotypes are based on our social ethic, which is to say our religion. As a result of stereotypes, the public believes that drug users are spineless, hedonistic criminals who should be jailed as quickly and for as long as possible. We thus describe the 99 percent of society (is there even 1 percent who have never taken an aspirin or a drug to feel better?) who are drug users and who are ourselves.

Marijuana was denounced in the 1930s because it was used by the outcasts of society—blacks, Mexicans, jazz musicians, and a few intellectuals—becoming a partial substitute for alcohol during Prohibition. It was associated with crime, violence, assassinations, and insanity, having been linked to the 1930s crime wave of Bonnie and Clyde, Ma Barker, and petty crooks who smoked marijuana, which was characterized as giving criminals a feeling of false courage and freedom from restraint. The prohibition of marijuana drove it underground, attracting more users. Law enforcement lumped marijuana use with heroin addiction, and penalties escalated. Billions of dollars are still being spent to stamp out marijuana use.

Drug stereotypes have no connection with reality or the physiological effect of a particular drug. The Drug Enforcement Administration has repeatedly refused to reclassify marijuana as other than a Schedule I drug, which it defines as "having no currently accepted medical use and a high potential for abuse." This prevents marijuana or any of its derived cannabinoids from being made available for medical use, though the DEA has turned a blind eye to use in states that have approved medical or recreational marijuana, which total two-thirds of the states. The façade began to crumble in 2018 when the Food and Drug Administration approved Epidiolex, which is derived from the marijuana molecule.

The National Institute on Drug Abuse reported in 2018 that substance abuse costs over $600 billion a year, a stupendous sum that could be greatly reduced by drug addiction treatment, for which there is little to no money budgeted. Treatment of a heroin addict (a year of methadone) costs about $4,700 per patient while a year in prison ranges from $24,000 to $30,000 for each convict. The Institute estimates that every dollar invested in treatment returns "between $4 and $7 in reduced drug-related crime, criminal justice costs, and theft. When saving related to healthcare are included, total savings can exceed costs by a ratio of 12 to 1. Major savings to the individual and to society also stem from fewer interpersonal conflicts; greater workplace productivity; and fewer drug-related accidents, including overdoses and deaths."

A report by the Global Commission on Drug Policy found that the number of Americans imprisoned for drug offences "has risen from approximately 38,000 to more than 500,000 in the last four decades. The lost productivity of this population was estimated by the [US Office of National

Drug Control Policy] in 2004 at approximately $40 billion annually."

Police payoffs and corruption are routinely linked to major drug deals. The executive director of the Police Executive Research Forum, which represents law enforcement agencies, says, "There's no question the numbers [of corrupt police officers] are increasing." Drug dealers consider police payoffs a cost of doing business. The sheriffs of counties in Oklahoma, Kentucky, South Carolina, Illinois, Texas, and Mississippi were indicted and convicted of drug trafficking over the last fifteen years.

In an average week in 2018 a Florida sheriff's deputy was arrested for stealing drug-buy money, with thirty-three separate incidents over the last year; in Maryland a former state prison guard was sentenced to three years in prison for accepting bribes to smuggle drugs into the prison, a conspiracy involving eighteen jailers and prisoners; and in Massachusetts a state prison guard was sentenced for smuggling opioids for an inmate. The UN 2017 *World Drug Report* concluded: "The drug problem and corruption have a mutually reinforcing relationship. Corruption facilitates the production and trafficking of illegal drugs and this, in turn, benefits corruption. The wealth and power of some drug trafficking organizations can exceed that of local governments, allowing them to buy protection from law enforcement agents, criminal justice institutions, politicians and the business sector. In doing so, they further reinforce corruption. The rule of law is both an immediate victim and, if it is already weak, an underlying factor that feeds this cycle."

Would anyone remain untempted if offered one million dollars to let a truck through a border checkpoint without inspection? One longtime customs agent, Rick Ashby, described the frustration:

"My guys work so damn many hours that their overtime comes out to about 50 cents an hour. They're tired and sleepy most of the time. Hell, who wouldn't be if you spent about half your nights sleeping out in the desert waiting for some bastard to come along with a load of dope? Then, when they bust somebody, they walk into a house with four Mercedes-Benz cars in the driveway, two or three 40-inch TVs in the house, and dinnerware that is made out of gold, not silver. And sometimes, there's so damn much money laying around that you have to have machines to count the stuff. Now, if you're a customs agent or any other kind of cop whose house is mortgaged to the hilt, and whose kids need braces, and whose old lady is threatening to leave because you've been too busy to take her on a vacation for the past three years, the scene can be tempting, even if it's just for a minute."

By 2017 the Mexican drug war was the third deadliest conflict on earth, behind only the Syrian Civil War and the battle against ISIS. In the first eleven months of 2017 the Mexican war had resulted in 23,101 murders including 11 journalists assassinated and thousands of Mexican citizens gone missing. The Mexican drug cartels are estimated to make between $13 billion and $49 billion from drug traffic to the U.S. alone, controlling 90 percent of the cocaine smuggled into the U.S.; cartel kingpins rank among the world's most powerful and richest individuals.

Arguably the most serious problem associated with the illegal cocaine trade is its destruction of the world's rain forests, particularly in the Amazon basin, and the dumping of millions of tons of toxic wastes, which result from the refining of cocaine, into the drainage areas of the Amazon highlands and headwaters. Five hundred thousand acres of tropical forests were destroyed and 1.5 million acres deforested by 1991, with coca plantations growing sevenfold since 1975 to meet U.S. demand for cocaine. By 2018 the deforestation had reached a point where the rain forest may change from tropical to a degraded savanna with low biodiversity because the Amazon system generates half of its own rainfall, which is dropping below sustainability and was exacerbated by the mega-droughts of 2005, 2010, and 2015–16. This threatens the water supply for Bolivia, Brazil, Colombia, Ecuador, and Peru, and many species may become extinct.

No government is equipped to prevent this destruction,

because the area is immense, rural, and controlled by drug cartels and settlers intent on clearing land for agriculture. Until drugs are legalized, removing the enormous illegal profits from the drug cartels, these areas are as uncontrollable and dangerous as Syria or Afghanistan. The cultivation of coca strips the soil and causes widespread erosion, with large portions of the Tingo Maria, Cutervo, and Abiseo national parks, and the Alexander Von Humboldt and Apurimac national forests largely destroyed. Until the drug trade is wrested from the cartels these areas cannot be preserved, and the lungs of the earth may gradually disappear, along with the atmosphere. The legalization of drugs is urgent, not merely the theoretically best thing to do as a solution to a wasteful drug war.

The Price of Punishing Victimless Behavior

One reason we don't understand drugs is because instead of getting our information from medical experts and pharmacologists it instead comes from law enforcement and politicians, who know as little as the general population. The use of alcohol and tobacco by our politicians and opinion makers has converted our two most used and dangerous drugs into sacred cows, which removes them from rational scrutiny and comparison with other drugs.

Congress has gradually stiffened its resolve to retard the use of tobacco, doubling the excise tax to $0.16 a pack in 1982, requiring warning labels in 1984, banning radio and television advertising, and prohibiting smoking on short airline flights in 1987, with the restriction extended to most flights in 1989. Excise taxes on cigarettes were 44 percent of the retail price by 2016. Since 2002, forty-eight states and the District of Columbia have increased cigarette tax rates 136 times. Still, the $120 billion–a-year tobacco industry remains a powerful lobby, and Congress is hesitant to move too quickly, recognizing the logrolling necessary and the number of votes wielded by tobacco states.

The war on drugs has perverted our government into "big brother" at a cost we have not yet begun to realize. We now believe it necessary to warn adults that anything they do may be dangerous to themselves or others, posting warnings on items that everyone knows to be dangerous such as cigarettes, alcohol, and swimming without a lifeguard. The human race was produced by survival of the fittest, evolving to a level where we seek to tell its members precisely what they can and cannot do though their behavior potentially harms no one but themselves. We are expending our resources in protecting the weak against themselves, with the risk that evolutionary progress will end while our basic freedom to be left alone evaporates.

Why should we imprison people who use any drug in moderation, harming no one, not even themselves? Why should we imprison people who use drugs to excess, harming no one directly but themselves? We don't criminalize any other behavior that harms no one else, except those few crimes commonly known as victimless.

Psychological dependence isn't restricted to drugs; it exists for all the important and pleasurable things in our lives—coffee, tea, cola, tobacco, alcohol, sports, television, phone screens, and sex. If you lose your phone or the television burns out, the family becomes irritable and restless, the same as anyone deprived of morning coffee, cocaine, or alcohol.

We can't afford the resources or loss of basic freedoms necessary to stop everyone from doing anything that may indirectly harm someone else. That would require criminalizing most foods we like because they contain an excess of fat, salt, and sugar, which will eventually kill us, indirectly harming our friends and relatives, parents, and children.

If we judge a drug, food, or activity based on its addictiveness and proclivity to waste time, our worst addiction is to our screens, whether TV or phone, which most are fully addicted to. It's the hearth around which we gather and no longer communicate. By 2018 Americans spent an average of eleven hours a day "listening to, watching, reading or generally interacting with media," according to the Nielsen Total Audience Report. The more we watch our screens, the more depressed, sadder, lonelier, hostile, and irritable we become. The psychiatric diagnostic manual defines addiction as compulsive and difficult-to-control behavior, which includes the social media and television-viewing habits of millions.

Our screens also promote obesity, particularly in children. An Auburn University study of 6,000 male viewers concluded that fatter and less fit men spend more time watching television. Those watching three or more hours a day were twice as likely to be obese as those watching an hour or less. Worse results were found for children. Children watching four or more hours of television a day are four times as likely to have high cholesterol levels as children watching two hours a day, according to research reported to the American Heart Association, based on a study of 1,077 suburban Southern California children.

A war against our screens may be more deserving than a war against drugs. By 2018 adult obesity in the U.S. had increased to 40 percent of the population (up from 15 percent in the 1970s). CDC data shows that obesity "increases the risk of developing type 2 diabetes, high blood pressure, heart disease, stroke, arthritis, sleep apnea, liver disease, kidney disease, gallbladder disease, and certain types of cancer." These diseases are far more serious than the harm caused by all illegal drugs.

The war on drugs is a war on ourselves. An Associated Press poll found that casual drug users in the United States, who don't use drugs to the point that would prevent them from holding a regular job, are estimated to number 25 million. They work with us every day without us knowing that they use illegal drugs any more than we would know whether they had drunk a beer, a glass of wine, or a mixed drink the night before.

* * *

The United States is the world's most repressive nation when it comes to imprisoning its citizens. In 2017 we spent $80 billion—more than $31,000 per inmate—to imprison one million people. About 300,000 of them were in prison solely because they possessed or sold drugs. Locking up drug offenders costs taxpayers enough to pay for universal healthcare or universal vocational or higher education.

In 2018 Bangladesh approved a draft law to impose the death penalty for drug offenses, mostly aimed at meth users, while Saudi Arabia executed 48 people for nonviolent drug crimes. Also in 2018 President Trump suggested the death penalty or life in prison for drug dealers, saying he got the idea from Singapore and China. He congratulated President Duterte in the Philippines for declaring open season on drug dealers, a policy that has resulted in thousands of vigilante-style deaths, revenge killings, and the deaths of innocent bystanders.

The American experiment with prohibition has faded from the memories of those now alive. Federal laws forbade alcohol except for "medicinal" or religious use but imposed no penalties for buyers, users, or possessors. Bootleggers received stiff fines for the first offense and six months in jail and a ten-thousand-dollar fine for the second offense. State laws, on the other hand, imposed brutal penalties for possession. In its eleven years of existence, the Prohibition Bureau hired 17,972 employees, fired 11,982 without cause, and terminated 1,604 for bribery, extortion, theft, falsification of records, forgery, and perjury. Journalist Franklin P. Adams described the Prohibition Commission under President Hoover:

It's left a trail of filth and slime;

It's filled the land with vice and
crime;

It don't prohibit worth a dime.

By 1930, a third of all federal inmates were incarcerated for alcohol offenses. The only difference between alcohol and illegal drugs is public opinion. If an alien were to read about the war on drugs and learn that legal drugs kill seventy-five people for each person killed by illegal drugs, what argument would prove our sanity?

As stated by Spinoza:

"All laws which can be violated without doing anyone any injury are laughed at. Nay, so far are they from doing anything to control the desires and passions of men that, on the contrary, they direct and incite men's thoughts the more toward those very objects; for we always strive toward what is forbidden and desire the things we are not allowed to have. And men of leisure are never deficient in the ingenuity needed to enable them to outwit laws aimed to regulate things which cannot be entirely forbidden. He who tries to determine everything by law will foment crime rather than lessen it."

Spinoza could have been describing the war on drugs.

* * *

We are quick to define a social problem as something that displeases us and to seek a remedy through the criminal justice system, which is an expensive method of making things worse for society. Simply because one or more religions deem victimless behavior as sinful doesn't mean the behavior should be criminalized.

It's immoral to punish victimless crimes. The "criminal" doesn't see himself as a victim, which makes rehabilitation difficult if not impossible. Instead of becoming rehabilitated, the "criminal" diligently avoids being caught in the future. In all other crimes there is a prosecuting witness or victim, without which the crime is almost never prosecuted. This is true of crimes from assault and battery to property crimes. Why should a person be viewed as a victim when he does not so view himself? Consensual private behavior of adults should be no business of the state or the criminal justice system. Does the Declaration of Independence guarantee life, liberty, and the pursuit of happiness, except when a dominant superstition disapproves of a particular victimless crime?

Criminalizing victimless crimes harms society because these "crimes" take more effort and money to prosecute without a witness, unless the witness is an undercover police officer. Police must hire witnesses, informers, and decoys, employ wiretaps and illegal searches, invade the privacy of others, spend billions of dollars, and still be almost completely ineffective. Without informers and decoys, prosecution of illegal drug crimes, prostitution, and gambling can't happen.

Victimless crimes (including drug possession for personal use, but excluding sales of drugs) are considered a joke by the vast majority of those in the legal system. Ask any prosecutor, judge, police officer, or defense lawyer, off the record. Few believe these crimes are evil. Hookers are back on the street in an hour. If they were a little higher class and more expensive, they'd never be busted in the first place; i.e., if they were hookers catering to prosecutors, judges, and defense attorneys. Most police aren't paid well enough to afford expensive hookers, except for the police assigned to victimless crimes who can make big-time bribe money. The purpose of these laws is a sop to public morality, which is morality codified before the Dark Ages, also known as hypocrisy.

Victimless crimes provide the primary opportunity for police corruption. There are more laws governing our behavior than the human mind can comprehend. As the number of laws escalates, so does the difficulty of enforcing them, with the result that individual police have increasingly unreviewable discretion to choose which laws to enforce and whom to arrest.

Victimless crimes encourage class discrimination. People with money are seldom arrested for these types of crimes. The privacy of the rich is far more secure than that of the poor. The result is disrespect for the criminal justice system and no deterrence. Is artificial religious morality worth the cost?

If Victimless Crimes Were Legalized

There are three main arguments against decriminalizing victimless crimes. The first argues that a victim is harmed. The answer is that society has no business telling adults what to do, whether they harm themselves or not. If we were to seek avoidance of self-harm as a goal, we would have to outlaw skiing, watching screens excessively, eating chocolate and other foods high in fat, salt, or sugar, driving cars, and especially smoking tobacco and drinking alcohol. Criminalization of these and other dangerous activities, however, harms the self/victim far more than not criminalizing the behavior.

The second argument is that without criminalizing the behavior, society would be encouraging it. This is an argument for children and for paternalism. Is it equally true that because we don't criminalize having sex with one hundred sex partners at once that we're encouraging orgies? Adults should be allowed to make their own choices as long as they harm no one else. No one needs to tell us what is good for us. If we can't decide that for ourselves, we don't exist as adults.

What others may see as a lack of will power may be our main pleasure in life. What right does society have to deny us that pleasure if we harm no one else when doing it? We primarily criminalize those acts that are contrary to the tenets of the locally dominant religion, aka superstition.

The criminal justice system should never be used to register social disapproval. This kind of symbolism has no deterrent effect and may instead increase criminal behavior; prohibition of those things that harm no one else is the mark of a bully.

The last argument is that morality demands criminalization. Morality demands only that something not be done, not that we be thrown in jail for doing it, unless it harms someone else. Only the arbitrary, man-made criminal justice system, fashioned from the collective wisdom of legislators, criminalizes behavior. The criminalization of victimless crimes is the imposition of the majority's religious beliefs on the minority and invades the privacy of adults.

Incarceration should be limited to those who harm others or another's property. Criminalizing victimless crimes trivializes violence and injury to others. Sending a possessor of marijuana to jail for a year when the penalty for killing another human being in negligent circumstances, such as when driving a car under the influence of alcohol, is also a year in jail, trivializes the killing of another human being. Sentencing a drug seller to ten years in prison for selling cocaine to his broker, or any other consenting adult, trivializes second-degree murder, which carries the same penalty. We point to capital punishment as the severest penalty, usually reserved for heinous murder or treason, though many would impose death for selling illegal drugs that are less dangerous than our legal drugs.

Advocates of criminal penalties for drug use argue that drug users need and use more public medical resources, costing society more in taxes. But those costs are infinitesimal compared to the cost of police, prisons, public defenders, prosecutors, judges, and the productive time lost by drug users who spend years in prison. Control advocates argue that drug use causes crime, but far more crime is caused by criminalizing drug use and driving it underground so that drug dealings must be made with organized criminals or other potentially violent entrepreneurs. The enforcement of drug laws takes its toll by raising the price of drugs so that users may resort to secondary crimes, which, unfortunately, are potentially violent crimes. Control advocates also argue that drug use leads to the neglect of families, but the criminal justice system causes far more familial neglect by putting mom or dad in prison. The fact that alcohol is legal often causes more familial neglect than all illegal drugs combined, but those supporting the war on drugs ignore this fact. The user neglects the family because alcohol is used excessively, which is the fault of the user, not the fault of the alcohol, which is the same for any drug and unrelated to whether the use of alcohol is legal or illegal.

Adults are the best judges of their own interests. We're more qualified to determine what is best for ourselves than state legislators and Congress and city councils and county boards of supervisors and the United Nations combined. Paternalism stultifies and renders adults less able to care themselves. What is best for the individual cannot effectively be written into unbending laws. Codification equals stultification and an inability to change. Experimentation and risk-taking is retarded, and progress slows. The whole basis for evolution and improvement of the species disappears when what is considered "right" at a particular moment is codified into the concrete of unchanging laws and religions.

Government paternalism is the same as tyranny. There is no act that harms no one else that is so dangerous that the public has a right to forbid it. Otherwise, we should uniformly, and without hypocrisy, forbid adults to harm themselves, whether the harm arises from alcohol, operating highly dangerous machinery (cars, planes, and implements used in dangerous sports), eating foods high in fat, salt, and cholesterol, or our illegal drugs. Then adults would be forbidden to do anything which is not good for them and compelled under the threat of criminal sanction to do those things that are good for them. For instance, all citizens would be required to meet at the track every morning at six A.M. for their morning exercise, television and smart phones would be highly restricted, only foods with high fiber content and low fat and cholesterol could be eaten. Hang-gliding, rock climbing, auto racing, driving in L.A., skiing, sky diving, and any dangerous activity would be forbidden. Adults would henceforth refrain from risking harm to themselves or they would go directly to jail.

Those who enjoy dangerous activities assume the risk of those activities, whether drug use or mountain climbing. If a person uses drugs or climbs mountains without considering the risks, the person is foolish and unworthy of protection. But why should foolish people be punished twice, once by the consequences of their behavior and then by being imprisoned? What is the logic of punishing people for harming themselves?

The Special Status of Minors

Children should be stringently protected against exposure to any drug, legal or illegal, unless medically necessary. Legal and illegal drugs delay and hinder maturation, preventing the child from learning responsible behavior. Drug use exacerbates the problems of adolescence and may keep the child from becoming a responsible adult. Teenagers using drugs are three times as likely to commit suicide as those not using drugs; suicide is the second-leading cause of death among fifteen-to twenty-nine-year-olds globally.

The most popular illegal drug among teens is marijuana, which is severely debilitating in a learning situation. The most popular legal drug is alcohol, which is similarly debilitating. As central nervous system depressants, alcohol and marijuana cause depression and, thus, make the user more susceptible to suicide. Those using central nervous system stimulants, such as cocaine, become depressed after dissipation of the high. After a crack binge there's an "almost intolerable" depression, which may encourage suicide. Alcohol, tobacco, barbiturates, sedatives, narcotics, central nervous system depressants, and tranquilizers should not be available to children under other than medically necessary circumstances.

A study released in 2018 by the National Institute on Drug Abuse for Teens found that teenagers have gotten the message about how dangerous our legal and illegal drugs are, except for marijuana, the use of which stays relatively steady. Though we're educating teens about illegal drugs the use of alcohol has risen.

Tobacco use, however, has dropped precipitously from almost 29 percent in 1974 to less than six percent in 2015. Fewer teens smoked nicotine than smoked marijuana. Unfortunately, the 2018 vaping craze has teens mesmerized by JUUL, a popular e-cigarette that looks like a thumb drive, using it at parties, when they drive, all the time. It's rechargeable by USB in an hour and comes in the flavors we love: cool mint, crème brulee, fruit medley, marketed as a safe alternative to cigarettes, though health officials fear they'll get teens hooked on high levels of nicotine.

A Question of Liberty

The war on drugs produces a war mentality; anything goes on both sides. Yet the sale of illegal drugs is as American as capitalism, a question of supply and demand. Why should the practitioners of capitalism, the guiding star of our economic system, be penalized because there's a demand for a product that directly harms no one but the user? Because we ignore this basic question, we've set ourselves up for abnegation of the Constitution and the radical expansion of a police state.

Seventy-three percent of Americans polled in 1990 said the U.S. Constitution guarantees the right to privacy from government interference with sex and that it allows them to withdraw life-support systems from the hopelessly ill. Seventy-three percent of Americans were flat wrong. Surveys show that 34 percent of us believe the "right of privacy" protects against random involuntary drug testing of employees. It, of course, does not. Privacy is mentioned nowhere in the Constitution. In rulings concerning birth control and abortion, the U.S. Supreme Court has inferred a limited right to privacy from the Fourteenth Amendment's "right to liberty" and the Fourth Amendment protection from unreasonable search and seizures, but conservative and liberal members of the court continually bicker over the existence of any privacy rights.

After President Bush's September 1989 drug speech, 62 percent of us said we'd give up basic civil liberties to help the war on drugs; by 2018 we had given up basic civil liberties to the extent that even an accusation of drug possession would allow the police to confiscate any property associated with illegal drug use or possession. How much freedom will we give up by 2030? Fifty-two percent would allow our homes to be searched without cause, and 67 percent would let our cars be stopped and searched at will, even if most searches found nothing. Eighty-two percent of citizens would allow the military to combat drugs in the United States, no matter the methods used. Fifty-five percent support drug testing for all Americans, 67 percent support testing for high-school students, and 83 percent for all drug users and their relatives, with reports going not to treatment centers but to the police. We would willingly sacrifice basic freedoms, enjoyed for over two hundred years, for a war against drugs that are less dangerous than our legal drugs of alcohol and tobacco

Although illegal drug use is dropping, drug testing has increased dramatically. In 1980, the number of firms testing was less than 10 percent. Today, 57 percent of major companies and 80 percent of aerodynamic and petroleum industry firms test applicants for drug use.

The central problems with drug testing are three: accuracy, enforced intrusion on privacy, and disclosure of use unrelated to impairment. A test that accurately shows an employee has used cocaine or marijuana doesn't show whether the employee has been impaired on the job, and a negative test result doesn't mean the employee hasn't been impaired on the job or didn't contribute to an accident. Unless a person is impaired on the job, there's no logical justification for drug testing. Even without drug testing, however, any supervisor should be able to tell whether an employee is impaired to the point of being unable to competently perform the job. Testing should be unnecessary for this purpose. There is no justification for drug testing when the comparative harm of legal and illegal drugs is considered and we fail to test for alcohol. Why should an individual be fired from a job if the person has never created a problem in the workplace and everyone is allowed to use the two most dangerous drugs with impunity?

The war on drugs has changed the presumption of innocence into a presumption of guilt. Both federal and state forfeiture laws provide for the summary seizure of cars, boats, and planes from people accused of drug offenses, whether they are convicted or not, and no matter the quantity of drugs found. A trace (usable amount) of any illegal drug is sufficient to require the forfeiture of the most expensive property, even if the property owner had no connection with the drug use. The Supreme Court has approved these seizures, though they may leave the accused with insufficient funds to hire counsel, with the result that the taxpayers must instead pay for an accused's attorneys. Justice Blackmun dissented in one such case, saying, "It is unseemly and unjust for the government to beggar those it prosecutes in order to disable their defense at trial." The American Bar Association said these decisions "seriously weaken our criminal justice adversarial system." This medieval system of confiscation was finally limited by the Supreme Court in 2019, requiring proportionality between the value of the drugs and the property seized, with no clear guidance on what this means.

The Supreme Court held on March 21, 1989, that the U.S. Customs Service could require mandatory urinalysis of all its employees, even though none were suspected of drug use, a decision applied to all branches of government over the next twenty-five years. The Customs Service sought these powers not because of suspected drug use but to showcase itself as an example of a drug-free workplace. Thus, the Fourth Amendment to the United States Constitution yielded to governmental symbolism, concerning which Justice Scalia wrote in his dissent, "The impairment of individual liberty cannot be the means of making a point. . .. Symbolism, even symbolism for so worthy a cause as the abolition of unlawful drugs, cannot validate an otherwise unreasonable search."

If the government can require urinalysis of anyone

without cause or reason, it can invade the privacy of any individual at its whim; the only pretext is the battle cry of a war on drugs. How long will it be before the police are allowed to search our homes without cause to see whether we use illegal drugs? Associate justice John Paul Stevens described how far the court has gone:

> "An extraordinarily aggressive Supreme Court has reached out to announce a host of new rules narrowing the federal Constitution's protection of individual liberties. The prosecutor's use of a coerced confession—no matter how vicious the police conduct might have been— may now constitute harmless error. The Court condoned the use of mandatory sentences that are manifestly and grossly disproportionate to the moral guilt of the offender. It broadened the powers of the police to invade the privacy of individual

citizens and even to detain them without any finding of probable cause or reasonable suspicion."

In 2019 President Trump announced that drug forfeiture money would be used to build his wall with Mexico because it would stop drugs coming into the United States (though they are primarily smuggled through legal ports of entry). When illegal drugs are available in prisons with four walls, razor wire, armed guards, and attack dogs, the efficacy of this reasoning may be suspect.

Under 23 U.S. Code 159, 10 percent of federal highway funds must be withheld from those states that fail to impose at least a six-month driver's license suspension for a drug possession conviction; its jurisdiction includes the 33 states where possession of marijuana, medical or recreational, is legal. Thirty-eight states have opted out of the highway-funding program because the law creates serious barriers to reentry into society. Still, every year 200,000 driver's licenses are revoked for possession of illegal drugs, mostly marijuana.

Half the states enforce their drug laws with tax penalties similar to those used in the prohibition era. When a person is arrested for possession or sale of illegal drugs, fines can be imposed and collected immediately, before conviction, and are kept even if criminal charges are later dropped or the accused is found innocent. Law enforcement spokesmen say, "The drug tax is one of the best pieces of anti-narcotics legislation to have come along in years." (Less than 5 percent of illegal drugs are narcotics.) To avoid the tax, an accused has the burden of proving unawareness of the drug; there is no presumption of innocence. And a negative cannot be proven.

In 1990 West Virginia newspapers began printing coupons for anonymously implicating neighbors and associates suspected of using illegal drugs. When the small-town Williamson newspaper printed a coupon, police received seven hundred responses listing names, addresses, or license-plate numbers of those suspected by their neighbors. Police arrested forty-six people during the first month. The state police immediately announced their own coupon campaign. The ACLU responded: "It creates a paranoid atmosphere, just the way it was in Germany in the '30s and '40s, when people were encouraged to spy on their neighbors. It's the thing going on today in Romania and Albania, where people complained to their government about the sense of always being watched. This kind of program will not make us drug-free. It will just make us unfree."

In 2014 the DEA launched an anonymous tip line that let anyone text the New England office to report illegal drug activity. All you have to do is text Tip411 (847411) and report your neighbor or anyone you don't like and the DEA will investigate. A year after the 2014 provision that ended the federal government's prohibition on medical marijuana, raids on medical marijuana dispensaries by federal agents continued in California. The California DEA stated, "We use power bills, water bills, informants, and we even track shipments by the United Parcel [Service] and other services from known suppliers to growers. We also do infrared imaging to check on the heat emitted from homes or warehouses we suspect." The DEA traces shipments of small greenhouses a few feet square. Don't send off for that attractive glass container to grow marigolds or you risk the DEA splintering your front door.

Mother Jones and *Playboy* magazines published the DEA's "scientifically tested profile" of suspected illegal drug users and dealers for interdiction at airports, bus stations, and on highways. The list may sound similar to that used during the various Inquisitions: carrying an old suitcase, a new suitcase, or a gym bag; driving a rental car or a car that contains air-freshener; taking an "evasive and erratic path" through the airport or scrupulously observing traffic laws; wearing a black jump suit or gold chains; traveling to or from Miami, Los Angeles, or Detroit; being a member of "ethnic groups associated with the drug trade"; appearing nervous or overly calm; buying one-way or round-trip tickets; traveling alone or with a companion; and deplaning from the front, middle, or rear of an aircraft.

The right of privacy should be preeminent so that every person has a guaranteed sanctuary from government or other interference. Only in public should an individual's acts be restricted because of the sensibilities of others. In private, people should be allowed—without restriction—to peruse whatever writings or pictures they wish, whether pornographic or religious (excluding those things that harm children, such as child pornography), to drink or imbibe drugs as they wish, and to do as they please sexually, as long as they harm no one else. On this theory of privacy, the Alaska Supreme Court held that private drug use is not subject to criminal penalties, but no other U.S. court has followed this precedent.

The majority of constitutional violations and intrusions on personal privacy occur in connection with the enforcement of drug laws. Three fourths of all search warrants are issued to support drug cases, primarily for wiretaps and electronic surveillance under the official designation of "organized crime." There's probably no crime less organized than drug dealing, except when run by the Mafia. Non-Mafia drug trafficking is done mostly by minority entrepreneurs who are able to get a cut of the capitalistic pie in few other ways. By searching airwaves, telephone conversations, and places of abode, we ignore basic rights of privacy for the purpose of imprisoning someone who is risking harm to no one but himself, or selling to someone who is paying for the privilege of risking harm to himself. Why should the Fourth Amendment prohibition against unreasonable intrusions on personal privacy and the Fifth Amendment right against self-incrimination be routinely compromised by the police to stop someone from risking harm to self, particularly when harm seldom results? This is the epitome of immorality.

Conclusion: Harm No One Else

[The basis for religion is] the haunting fear that someone,
somewhere, may be happy.
—H. L. Mencken

Acts historically considered criminal have included sacrilege, blasphemy, denial of the existence of God, refusal to swear an oath, and hundreds of other religion-related acts. The only reason that acts harming no one else are still criminalized is religion and the vestiges of religious "logic" that permeate our society. Heresy was subject to the death penalty because a society tolerating heresy was believed to be subject to death from the deity, which in its displeasure could destroy the community in retribution for the community's failure to execute the heretic. If a particular community's deity, however, has lost the ability to destroy the community there's no justification for prohibiting acts in private that harm no one else. Drugs are criminalized because our legislatures feel that drugs destroy the moral fiber of the community, which is the same as saying the deity disapproves of drugs. Simply put, the war on drugs is a continuation of the various religious crusades and inquisitions that bedeviled the world for eight hundred years, continuing unabated in the Middle East and Africa.

Morality and ethics are not dependent on punishment

or reward but exist independently, without any necessary connection with organized religion. The human need to believe in something, whether rational or baseless, and to respond more to wishes, desires, hopes, and fears than to facts, results in a delusion of self. Why do so many of us reject the present and the only life we know for certain, instead relying on the unknown and unknowable for an ephemeral promise of immortality? The tragedy of religion is its ability to delude people into thinking misery on earth will buy eternal paradise. Those living under the illogical and archaic rules of religion are under a dictator the same as those living under a communistic totalitarian regime with mind police on every corner. We must confess our "sins." Can there be a universally objective definition of "sin" other than harming another? If so, what is it and what is the moral basis for categorizing any act, other than an action harming another, as sinful?

The meaning of life without the illusion of immortality is personal responsibility. When religion (or government, or any entity other than ourselves) is the decision-maker, there can be no personal responsibility, only childish paternalism.

Because of religion, our schools are propaganda machines occupied more with questions of creationism, religious studies, sex education, and prayer than with education. True education is not allowed in our schools. Never will the public schools teach evolution without creationism, the facts of science without the myths of religion, the facts of the inherent barbarity and close-mindedness of religion as illustrated by the various Inquisitions and the Crusades, the internal illogic of the concept of "God," or the irrationality of the origins of religion in the fears and superstitions of primitive humans. The primary purpose of the public schools (and especially religious schools) appears to be indoctrination, not education. Where religion governs, thinking for oneself, which is the goal of education, becomes heresy, because religion deems its dogma as absolute truth.

Religion and morality are antithetical and contradictory. Not only is religion unnecessary to morality, but religion is immoral insofar as it teaches there is no other truth except within the narrow dictates of a particular faith. Real morality is learned from the observation of parents, peers, and teachers, not by artificial religious rules , concocted before the Dark Ages, that have little connection with reality. Instead of teaching that no one else should be harmed, religion teaches that those having other beliefs should be slaughtered or converted. This is the opposite of morality and is instead the epitome of evil.

The pluralism of the United States is threatened by religion and religious thought. The purpose of the checks and balances of constitutional government is to prevent the enslavement of minorities by the majority. The idea that the

United States is a Christian nation defeats this central principle, making any non-Christian, whether Jewish, Buddhist, Muslim, or atheist, a nonentity. The stultification of pluralism is immoral. Which is more moral and ethical: religious absolutism teaching the slaughter or conversion of nonbelievers, or a recognition that all humans are essentially the same, with similar fears, needs, and aspirations, requiring tolerance and acceptance of other viewpoints?

* * *

Life is not meaningless without religion. Without religion there is still success in work and profession, achievement, love, creativity, reason, the helping of others, and the improvement of society. Religion fosters guilt, demeans self-worth, and prohibits acts that harm no one else while the concept of sin varies radically among our thousands of religions. When the fact of death is hidden by religious dogma, human potential remains unfulfilled because there's no incentive for improving this life. We should choose life, not an unseeable and vaporous god whose concept is illogical and nonsensical.

Religion seeks to compensate for the lack of control over our lives and future by creating an illusion of control. Women, having less control over their lives, are more religious than men. Similarly, classes of society that have less control over their lives are more religious. The less individual control we have, the lower and poorer our social class, the higher the incidence and intensity of religion. A rich man fails to enter the kingdom of heaven because he has no need to.

The negatives of organized religion include its authoritarianism, which retards thought and constitutes an opiate of the masses, the same as any drug or addiction. Religion is the defender of the status quo and of the government in power, no matter the morality or corruption of the government. Render unto Caesar that which is Caesar's. Religion controls government from within, which is easier than competing with government for ascendance. Consider Mexico, Guatemala, El Salvador, Panama, South America, Spain, Italy, and Greece. In its dealings with dictators and other terrorists, the church is to Christ as China is to Marx. Neither have the slightest connection, except by label. No authoritarian regime is defensible, whether in the former Soviet Union, or Argentina, or the Vatican. All require blind obedience on pain of death, whether physical death or death of the soul.

The concept of soul and immortality are unintelligible. There is no evidence to support the existence of either. The argument that immortality is necessary to justify morality is an argument for children. Belief in immortality is reality-avoidance based on the reluctance to face the inescapable reality of death. Why do the religious believe that the fear of damnation or the hope of immortality is a necessary basis for ethics and morality?

* * *

Religion opposes free inquiry because free inquiry leads to contradiction of the central tenets of all religions. Religion is also the expert on censorship, whether art, movies, or books. It's indistinguishable from superstition, where magic and myth are considered truth. It means blind conformity, moral hypocrisy, and enslavement of the individual to the fears of primitive humans. Many recently founded Christian sects are alive and growing, including the Seventh-day Adventists, Mormons, Christian Scientists, and the Unification Church of Reverend Moon. The Moonies are an example of a combination of New Age and Christian religions, with an emphasis on money and hoped-for wealth for its members. The Unification Church claims three million members worldwide with 37,000 missionaries and lay members in the United States. Its growth slowed after Rev. Moon served twelve months of an eighteen-month sentence for tax evasion from 1984 to 1985. Thereafter, the church began giving free trips to South Korea for leaders of mainline U.S. churches. The Unification Church believes in Jesus and the Sermon on the Mount, but also believes that other Christian denominations haven't lived up to Jesus' teachings, which has been the cry of every reformed Christian group since the beginning of Christianity, and with good reason. Moon teaches that Jesus wasn't supposed to be crucified but came to earth as a second Adam to take a bride. Together, Jesus and his bride would become the "true parents," returning the human race to the paradise of the Garden of Eden. In a speech given by Rev. Moon in New Orleans, he explained the crucifixion of Jesus as "the result of the faithlessness of the Jewish people. The major cause of their faithlessness was the betrayal of John [the Baptist]. . . . You may again want to ask me, 'With what authority do you say these things?' I spoke with Jesus Christ in the spirit world. And I also spoke with John the Baptist."

All religions, new and old, are based in belief that runs contrary to logic, human dignity, and basic human rights. Their leaders, from Rev. Moon to Oral Roberts to the pope, have all claimed to personally talk with Jesus. They all require the conversion of heathens, bringing up children in the faith, prohibition of marriage outside the faith, and suppression of dissent.

The two most cited positives of religion are instead negatives:

(1) *Religion gives meaning and direction to life.* If the direction and meaning are false, based on superstition, and lead to a wasted life, is religion a positive factor?

(2) *Religion unifies society and imbues the culture with altruistic moral feelings and commonly shared goals.* If religious goals are based on superstition, and if moral goals are commonly shared worldwide regardless of religion, what

value is added by organized religion? Our first goal should be protection from each other and security of the individual. Other considerations should be subservient to preservation and safety of the individual as long as the individual harms no one else. Nations, states, classes of people, and religions are superficial "false karasses and grand falloons" without positive value but with dangerous hidden costs. Why is it unnatural to limit population by the voluntary practice of birth control in order to avoid starvation and poverty, to seek cures for disease, and to transplant human organs to save lives? The contradictions of religion are solvable only by a declaration of gullibility. Anyone who'd believe in a god would believe anything.

A major difficulty with accurately judging the morality of another's act is that we can never know all the circumstances that led to the act. Without full knowledge, judging others is unfair. For this reason alone, harming no one else appears to be the only absolute that can safely be applied to ourselves and to others. Under only one circumstance can we ethically harm another and that is in actual self-defense. We can, however, accurately judge the morality of our governments and religions because their flaws are openly displayed. Imagine the benefits of a system that would forbid harming another and forbid nothing else. The armies of the world could be disbanded, freeing up half the gross international product, raising the world standard of

325

living, eradicating 90 percent of childhood deaths, and protecting the environment for future generations. Neither self-interest nor the hedonistic pursuit of pleasure would carry negative connotations if preceded by a prohibition against harming others. We would achieve a morality made for humans instead of shoe-horning ourselves into a morality that doesn't fit, a morality imposed by the superstitions of our ancestors, which have been passed on to us in the form of organized and fallible religion.

* * *

Ethics consists of three principles: harming no one else, exercising personal responsibility, and relinquishing control over other adults. Without all three, ethics cannot exist.

Principle 1: Harm no one else, unless in actual self-defense. This is the core of ethics and morality. All else is secondary. No other ethical concept constitutes morality.

Our thousands of infallible religions and their symbiotic governments have been used by special interests to thwart this goal through the crippling of individual freedom and responsibility. Indeed, the institutions which should be most strictly guided by ethics have, in fact, been its greatest detractors. Accordingly, society would be better served by no organized religion at all and considerably less government.

Principle 2: No institution should be allowed to

control the adult individual as long as he harms no one else. Religion acts ethically only when it asserts no control over adult behavior that harms no one else. Controlling adults who harm no one else is paternalistic and stultifying.

Religions and the religious should be treated with the utmost tolerance, as should all of our kind, as long as they harm no one else. Religion can claim no connection to ethics and morality as long as it fails to obey this central ethical commandment. For organized religion, however, relinquishment of control over the individual would mean the end.

Seeking no control over adults is contrary to basic religious principles because the aim of religion is to control its members, their finances, and their sex lives. Religions seek control over education, science, sex, women, gays, government, and "them." Religions control "them" through conversion, missionaries, war, Crusades, and Inquisitions. This sought-after religious control pits the religious "us" against the other thousands of religions and the nonreligious "them." The general religious prohibition against birth control stems from the race for supremacy of our thousands of religions, resulting in the impoverishment of Africa, where every country is dominated by fundamentalist Christians, Muslims, or both.

Religion solicits money in exchange for immortality or nirvana. Most organized religion exists to relieve human anxiety about death. The first purpose of religion for our ancestors was to control the spirits and the unknown that surrounds us, to control the uncontrollable and the nonexistent. In return for a promise of immortality, Western religion demands our only asset—control over our life on earth. The purpose of this control has no connection with ethics or morality and in fact is unethical and immoral.

The positive siren of religion is man's search for goodness and ethics. When the concept of religion is separated from that of ethics, religion is of a vapid set of artificial dos and don'ts.

Principle 3: Only adults who accept full and unswerving responsibility for the consequences of their actions are entitled to do as they please. Personal responsibility and ethical behavior are synonymous. Without personal responsibility, which is simply control over ourselves by ourselves and not by others, there is no ethics. We should all bear the consequences of our acts or failure to act. Adults who harm others deserve incarceration and forced restitution to repay the harm caused to others. Only those adults who harm no one else are ethical and exercise personal responsibility.

Any adult who allows government to support him though he is able to support himself, or who religiously confesses harm to others and thereby feels absolved, has abdicated personal responsibility. Adult irresponsibility

328

fuels the growth of religion and interdependent governments.

Personal responsibility is acquired through education. Reliance on a god or incorporeal spirit is personally irresponsible. Children believe without proof or logic; adults should require proof and logic.

Religious rules promote irresponsibility because they instruct us to avoid education, except as contained in the "bible" of the particular religion, and to believe without proof or logic. Knowledge, including sex education, is the forbidden fruit that caused the downfall of man.

Personal responsibility extends to safeguarding our own health. Highly addictive drugs, such as tobacco and cocaine derivatives, should never be used because they're too dangerous, but their use should still be left up to the adult individual. Almost all other drugs can be used by most people in moderation and are relatively harmless to those who can control their use.

Whether adults wish to be controlled by religion is their business, as it should equally be the personal business of any adult whether to use legal or illegal drugs, enjoy sex of whatever consensual nature, watch their phone screens ten hours a day, work weekends and nights, or retire to the couch with pizza and French fries.

A minority will never be personally responsible, whether tempted by drugs, sex, or risk of any kind.

Personal responsibility is the basis for progress within ethical bounds. The exercise of personal responsibility defines the adult, while a prohibition against individual decision-making defines childhood. Adult freedom to make unrestricted decisions promotes our evolution and the survival of the fittest of our kind.

"Without a global revolution in the sphere of human consciousness, nothing will change for the better in the sphere of our being," said Vaclav Havel when, as president of Czechoslovakia, he addressed the U.S. Congress: "We still don't know how to put morality ahead of politics, science, and economy. We are still incapable of understanding that the only genuine backbone of all our actions, if they are to be moral, is responsibility.

"Responsibility to something higher than my family, my country, my company, my success -- responsibility to the order of being where all our actions are indelibly recorded and where and only where they will be properly judged.

"The interpreter or mediator between us and this higher authority is what is traditionally referred to as human conscience."

This higher calling is to the species, our kind, unswerving loyalty to the human race, above any lesser allegiances, such as those demanded by nations, religions, and race. Religion and government encourage and institutionalize the idea of us against them, which is unethical and immoral. We should reject the institutions that set us against ourselves, humans against humans. Nations and religions would do well to fade away so that only the necessary function of government, to prevent physical harm to its citizens and their property, remains. To accomplish this end, the pursuit of objective knowledge, as opposed to primitive superstition, should be available to and encouraged for all.

Our kind has always had ambitious goals, but we can be both ambitious and ethical. A maximum of individual freedom, constrained only by self-responsibility and the ethical principle of harming no one else, is the primary condition that will allow our kind to achieve its highest rational aspirations.

* * *

If you liked this book, please leave a review

Also by David Rich

Sail the World? – An Absurdly True Story, Prequel to RV the World

RV the World, 2nd Edition

Myths of the Tribe - When Religion and Ethics Diverge

Scribes of the Tribe - The Great Thinkers on Religion and Ethics

The ISIS Affair - Putting the Fun Back in Fundamentalism

Antelopes - A Modern Gulliver's Travels

Read on for an excerpt from *RV the World* by David Rich.

RV the World: An Excerpt

My earliest vivid memory is of a photo from an old geography book: Vesuvius in full-color eruption spewing fluorescent orange magma, torching rich Romans in Pompeii. This hit me between the eyes. Whoa. I really had to see that in person. What six-year-old wouldn't?

I could never kick this early memory, which evolved into a dream of seeing the world, the whole lot of it. My earliest ambition was finding the world's most fabulous volcanoes, my curiosity spurred by schoolteacher parents with a passion for travel and geography. I inherited a travel addiction, doomed to see the entire world or die trying.

I nagged my long-suffering parents to drive down every road, reasoning that we might stumble across Vesuvius anywhere. Humoring me, they drove down lots of dirt roads, many ending on the edges of deep canyons in Colorado, New Mexico, Utah, and Arizona, the Four Corners area where I grew up. They'd brought it on themselves, infecting me with a travel-and-geography obsession, insisting in return for my see-the-end-of-every-road harassment that I learn context, all the states, their capitals, and the capital of every country on the planet. I was crushed to find Vesuvius nowhere near the Four Corners.

An outlet for itchy feet fortuitously appeared when I was teaching at the local law school. A student said, "Hey, come help me try out my new sailboat." That day one of Arizona's many lakes became a scene of high comedy. By 10 a.m. we finally got the pole up. I later learned it was called a mast. Though we scooted down the lake in half an hour, downwind, it took until sunset to sail back as we cursed gods whose proper names we didn't know—the gods of tacking, coming about, and shifting winds. I was indelibly hooked.

After a few months of torture on my friend's Hobie Cat, including six crazy days sailing down the Mexican coast from Puerto Penasco to Bahia Kino, I finally enrolled—along with my wife, Mary—in a learn-to-sail course at the Annapolis Sailing School in San Diego. Then I tackled the advanced sailing course, which theoretically qualified me to bareboat charter.

Suddenly I wanted to sail around the world. People said, "But you live in Arizona. There's no water, except a few ridiculous lakes." By then everyone knew I'd gone stark raving mad—including Mary, but she gradually contracted the insatiable wanderlust encouraged by my parents.

I captained seventeen charters in Greece, Turkey, Vancouver, Belize, and most of the Bahamas and Caribbean Islands. It was my responsibility to find a proper sailing vessel (best price), set up the charter, organize disorganized friends during bouts of personal disorganization, and then, once we arrived at the destination, find water, fuel, and a likely place to moor or anchor each night. I halfway learned to sail a dozen different sailboats while my accompanying friends coughed up three hundred dollars per person for the pleasure of crewing. Aren't friends fabulous?

The second most glorious day of my life was buying a dreamboat to sail around the world. I named her Grendel. Mary and I spent years flying on weekends from Phoenix to San Diego, putting every toy aboard, from mast steps to radar to a water maker. The big day arrived when, after saving every penny on a ten-year plan that stretched to eleven years, I sold everything and sailed Grendel out of San Diego Harbor.

It became abundantly clear that Dave and Mary sailing around the world was not exactly as it appeared in Romancing the Stone when Michael Douglas and Kathleen Turner sailed into the sunset. No, life on Grendel was more about la problema del dia, the problem of the day, especially for someone who'd flunked grade school shop and was the least mechanically minded in the history of the Montezuma County public school system in Cortez, Colorado. To sail around the world you not only need to know how to sail but also how to fix stuff—all the stuff, including mechanical and electrical— and you need the baksheesh to coax replacement parts through foreign customs.

Hollywood had done me a disservice—or perhaps, like

those guys who count landing at an international airport as visiting a country, I was a dope. After a year we were still in Mexico, though far down the Pacific Coast. The Marquesas and Tuamotus islands were next on our itinerary, and as the specter of a thirty- to forty-day ocean crossing loomed closer, I faced up to my terminal ineptness with a multi-meter and a monkey wrench, and Mary admitted to hating unending oceans. A compulsive jogger, she found the deck was too small for laps. We turned north to San Diego, where I experienced my most glorious day, selling Grendel.

By no means was this the end of my dream of seeing the world but instead the true beginning. Living on a sailboat relegated us, two non-beach persons, to the coast, though 90 percent of what there is to see is inland. We found sailing the very best way to spend time fixing stuff in exotic ports, leaving little time for exploration.

We began international RVing in 1994. That year we flew to Germany and bought an RV with the proceeds from Grendel. We lived the next three years in forty countries, spending summers in the United Kingdom, Ireland, Norway, and Scandinavia and winters in Spain, Portugal, Morocco, Italy (where I finally saw Vesuvius not erupting), Greece, Turkey, Israel, Jordan, and Egypt, plus all the countries in between. Seventeen years later, though we have stopped full-time RVing, we're still RVing the world six months a year.

We've visited hundreds of scenic spots available

overnight only by tent or RV. Among our favorite experiences have been overnighting within or next to:

- The Horns of Hittite, where the Crusaders met their final demise above Lake Kinneret (aka the Sea of Galilee), where we were visited by a helicopter.

- New Zealand's Mount Cook, framed by our RV's panoramic windows, and Milford Sound, which we had all to ourselves after the tour buses had gone home for the night.

- A remote beach in New South Wales, where we were surrounded by kangaroos.

- The world's most incredible ruins at ancient Petra, and definitely by ourselves in remote Wadi Rum, where Larry of Arabia hung out, both in Jordan.

- Alice Springs in Australia's Northern Territory, where we watched a full eclipse of the moon atop our RV.

- The wind-hewn canyons of the Negev Desert. A French canal and an ancient French monastery in a primeval forest.

- Hobart Bay and Cradle Mountain in Tasmania. Purnululu National Park in the orange-and-black-striped mountains of the Bungle Bungles, and at the confluence of sandstone slot canyons in Karajini National Park, in Western Australia.

- The waterfront in Ushuaia, Argentina, the southernmost city in the world, where we watched ships leave for Antarctica, and in Tierra Del Fuego National Park, outside Ushuaia, at the foot of the last of the Andes, on the Beagle Channel.

- Vesuvius overlooking the bay and the lights of Naples.

- The canals of Bruges, Amsterdam, and Venice. (Unfortunately, the Chinese government prohibits driving an RV to the canals of Suzhou).

- Finland's many lakes, surrounded by reindeer. The waterfront in Stockholm, where we camped for a week.

- Lake Titicaca in Bolivia. Another Bolivian favorite is Mount Sajama (21,000 feet), where we camped at 15,000 feet next to hot springs a few kilometers from the border with Chile and a lake perfectly reflected twin Fuji-esque cones.

The week before I quit playing lawyer, several friends said they envied my plan. The brevity of life had been vividly illustrated to them. They, like me, had always treated life as if it went on forever. One guy's brother had been diagnosed with inoperable cancer, a month before his scheduled retirement. Another's father had prostate cancer, chose the operation, and died two weeks after retiring. Mary's boss had dreamed of buying an oceangoing fishing boat but kept putting it off. He needed to add to his retirement kitty. Just before we left he was diagnosed with a brain tumor and died a year later. Do it now, whatever it is you want to do. If we don't do it now, the odds are we never will. Perhaps along the way you'll find the world's most picturesque volcano.

www.ingramcontent.com/pod-product-compliance
Lightning Source LLC
Chambersburg PA
CBHW021134090426
42740CB00008B/784